T0004015

MO☽N

52 THINGS
TO DO IN

PHOENIX & TUCSON

JESSICA DUNHAM

CONTENTS

Phoenix

Day Trips and Getaways

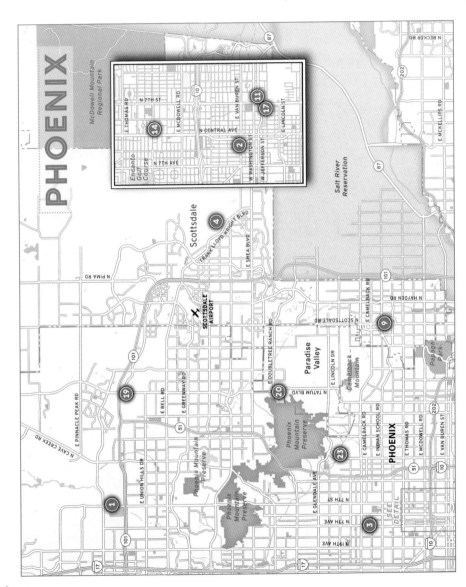

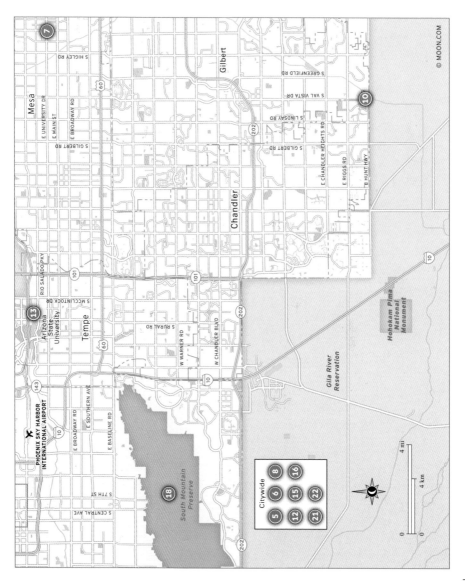

© MOON.COM

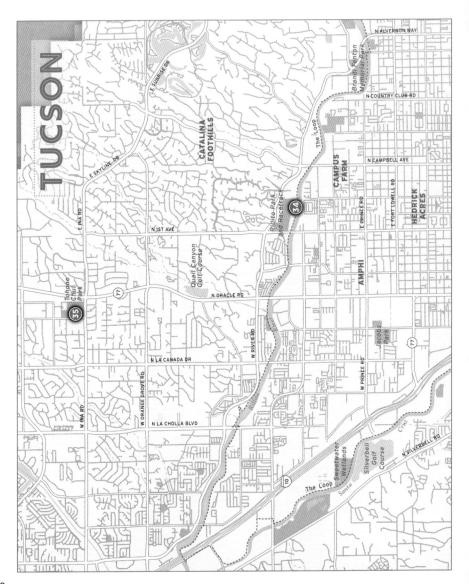

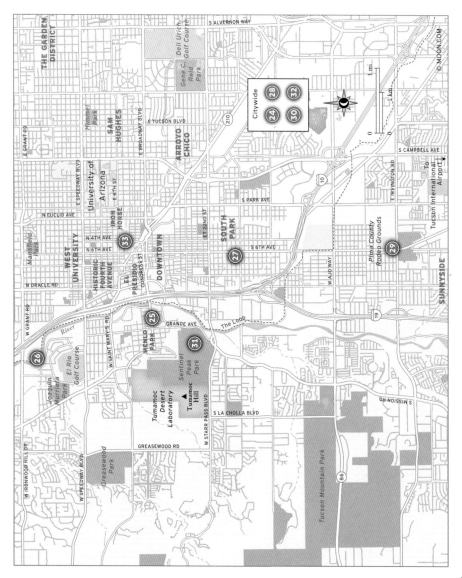

S ALVERNON WAY

THE GARDEN DISTRICT

Del Urich Golf Course

Gene C. Reid Park

© MOON.COM

Citywide

28 **32**
24 **30**

S CAMPBELL AVE

E GRANT RD

Himmel Park

SAM HUGHES

S TUCSON BLVD

ARROYO CHICO

To Tucson International Airport

E SPEEDWAY BLVD

University of Arizona

E 6TH ST

E BROADWAY BLVD

210

S PARK AVE

10

E IRVINGTON RD

N EUCLID AVE

Mansfield Park

WEST UNIVERSITY

N 4TH AVE

IRON HORSE

33

E 22ND ST

SOUTH PARK

Pima County Rodeo Grounds

29

N 6TH AVE

HISTORIC FOURTH AVENUE

EL PRESIDIO

CONGRESS ST

DOWNTOWN

S 6TH AVE

27

N ORACLE RD

N DRACLE RD

W GRANT RD

W AJO WAY

SUNNYSIDE

River

W SANTA MARY'S RD

GRANDE AVE

The Loop

19

25

26

El Rio Golf Course

MENLO PARK

31

Sentinel Peak Park

Joaquin Murrieta Park

Tumamoc Desert Laboratory

▲ Tumamoc Hill

S LA CHOLLA BLVD

S MISSION RD

W IRONWOOD HILL DR

GREASEWOOD RD

W STARR PASS BLVD

Greasewood Park

W SPEEDWAY BLVD

Tucson Mountain Park

86

0   1 mi

0   1 km

9

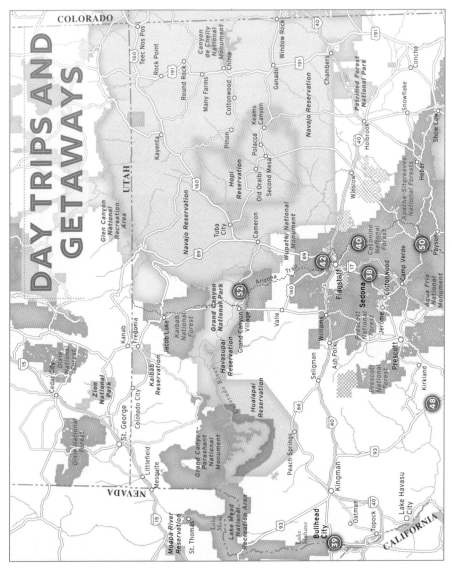

DAY TRIPS AND GETAWAYS

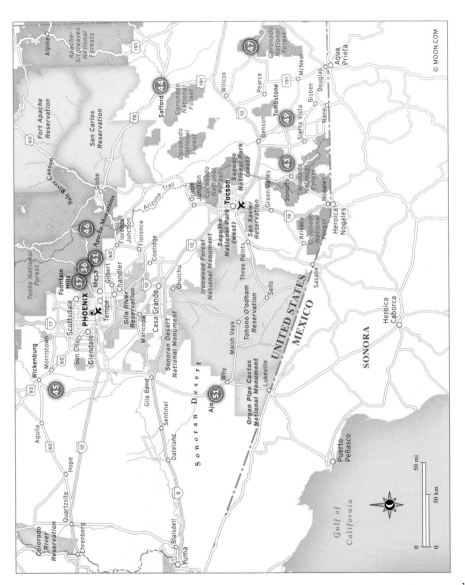

© MOON.COM

11

(RE)DISCOVER PHOENIX & TUCSON

Connected by the craggy beauty of the Sonoran Desert, Phoenix and Tucson are sister cities, thriving metropolises teeming with things to do and places to see.

First things first: When Phoenicians say "Phoenix," what we really mean is "the Valley," a cluster of neighboring communities whose borders bleed into one another. Each offers a unique highlight. The college town of Tempe is home to Miss Gay Arizona Pageant. The Fresh Foodie Trail threads through the farmlands of Gilbert, Mesa, and Queen Creek, granting a taste (literally) of Arizona's agritourism hub. The nation's Major League Baseball teams gear up for the season at spring training games in Scottsdale. And there's big-city Phoenix with its laid-back ways, where a James Beard Award-nominated chef like Silvana Salcido Esparza of Barrio Café cruises her neighborhood in a low-rider.

In Tucson, cycling is the preferred mode of transportation. Locals on two wheels take to the bike-friendly streets or ride The Loop, a paved path that surrounds the city. Tucsonans love a good party, too. The Return of the Mermaids festival celebrates the desert's monsoon season, while La Fiesta de Los Vaqueros (cowboy party) is a rodeo so beloved in town that adults take off work to attend and kids skip school to watch the parade. You'll find Mexican influences everywhere, from the Sonoran-style food to the street names.

Then there are the people. Many of us who live in Phoenix and Tucson came from somewhere else. We found our way to the desert for any number of reasons—better health, sunny days—and because of that, there's a lively energy among Phoenicians and Tucsonans of having discovered a second lease on life, a chance to start again, a do-over, perhaps. There's a sense that this scorched-in-the-sun place was *chosen*. It's not the home we were given—it's the home we made.

TO DO LISTS

Phoenix Essential

1 Take to the sky in a **hot-air balloon**

2 Cheer on *lucha libre* at Crescent Ballroom

3 Taste the **Fry Bread House's namesake dish**

4 Tour **Taliesin West**

10 Stretch out at **goat yoga**

12 Play hooky at a **Cactus League Spring Training** game

14 Learn about Arizona's **American Indian heritage** at the Heard Museum

15 Explore Phoenix's **mid-century modern architecture**

16 Celebrate the **Miss Gay Arizona America Pageant**

19 Play at the **Musical Instrument Museum**

Tucson Essential

Native Cultures

3 Taste the **Fry Bread House's namesake dish**

9 Buy authentic **American Indian art**

14 Learn about Arizona's **American Indian heritage** at the Heard Museum

28 Hunt for **murals**

51 Pick **saguaro fruit**

Local Scenes

2 Cheer on *lucha libre* at Crescent Ballroom

5 Discover **new writers** at local bookstores

8 Hear **local voices** at Arizona Storytellers Project

11 Feast on **soul food** at Mrs. White's Golden Rule Café

21 Dive into the **blues and R&B music scene**

22 **Shop** local

25 Honor the dead at the **All Souls Procession**

29 Join **La Fiesta de Los Vaqueros**

34 Stroll the **Heirloom Farmers Market** at Rillito Park

45 Haunt a **ghost town**

Beautiful Views

1 Take to the sky in a **hot-air balloon**

18 **Watch the sun set** at South Mountain Park

31 **Summit "A" Mountain** at sunrise

36 See **wild horses** along the Salt River

37 Helicopter over the **world's fourth-tallest fountain**

38 **Dine** in the desert

52 Join a **star party**

Rhythm Room mural by Curt Condrat

Art and Culture

4 Tour **Taliesin West**

5 Discover **new writers** at local bookstores

8 Hear **local voices** at Arizona Storytellers Project

9 Buy authentic **American Indian art**

14 Learn about Arizona's **American Indian heritage** at the Heard Museum

15 Explore Phoenix's **mid-century modern architecture**

16 Celebrate the **Miss Gay Arizona America Pageant**

19 Play at the **Musical Instrument Museum**

21 Dive into the **blues and R&B music scene**

Outdoor Adventures

13 Ply the waters of **Tempe Town Lake**

18 **Watch the sun set** at South Mountain Park

20 Lace up your boots for an **urban hike on Trail 100**

26 **Bike** the Loop

36 See **wild horses** along the Salt River

37 Helicopter over the **world's fourth-tallest fountain**

39 Dip into **hot springs**

42 Trek the **Arizona Trail**

46 Cool off in **secret swimming holes**

52 Join a **star party**

Fun for Families and Kids

⑩ Stretch out at **goat yoga**

⑰ Go behind the scenes at **sports stadiums**

⑲ Play at the **Musical Instrument Museum**

㉝ See **mermaids** on Fourth Avenue

㉞ Stroll the **Heirloom Farmers Market** at Rillito Park

㊴ Pack up for a **family campout**

㊼ Join a **star party**

Drink and Dine

3 Taste the **Fry Bread House's namesake dish**

6 Toast an **Arizona brew**

7 Take a field trip on the **Fresh Foodie Trail**

11 Feast on **soul food** at Mrs. White's Golden Rule Café

24 Taste Tucson's **global flavors**

30 Raise your glass in **historic bars**

32 Savor **Sonoran-style food**

38 **Dine** in the desert

43 Go **wine-tasting**

44 Follow the **Salsa Trail**

Shopping

⑤ Discover **new writers** at local bookstores

⑨ Buy authentic **American Indian art**

㉒ **Shop** local

㉗ Outfit yourself in **custom Western boots**

㉞ Stroll the **Heirloom Farmers Market** at Rillito Park

㉟ Transform your backyard with **desert plants**

Day Trips

37 Helicopter over the **world's fourth-tallest fountain**

41 Enjoy **desert blooms and autumn leaves**

43 Go **wine-tasting**

44 Follow the **Salsa Trail**

45 Haunt a **ghost town**

46 Cool off in **secret swimming holes**

48 Drive the **Joshua Tree Parkway**

50 Wander **lavender fields**

Weekend Getaways

1 Take to the sky in a hot-air balloon

Phoenix Essential • Beautiful Views • Outdoor Adventures

Why Go: There's something about drifting through a clear blue sky on a gentle air current, the Sonoran Desert sprawling in all directions, that grants you a little perspective.

Where: Rainbow Ryders, 715 E. Covey Lane, Ste. 100, 480/299-0154, www.rainbowryders.com

Timing: Balloon flights depart daily at dawn and dusk. Sunrise flights take off year-round, but sunset flights run November through March only. The experience takes about 3-4 hours, which includes travel to the launch site and back from the landing site; in-air time is about 45 minutes to 1 hour. Pack light layers and a camera. Most flights include bottled water, as well as a celebratory snack upon landing, so there's no need to pack food and drinks.

From any vantage point in metro Phoenix, if you're awake just as the sun's rays slice through the Four Peaks, you'll see dozens of brightly colored hot air balloons hovering in the north. Some fly high while others hang low, their people-filled baskets skirting the tops of palo verde trees and the roofs of houses.

How many places can claim hot air balloons as a fact of daily life, as commonplace as rush-hour traffic? Not many. As far as epic, bucket-list, once-in-a-lifetime experiences go, hot air ballooning tops the list *and* it's offered right here in our very own backyard. (Literally. One time a hot air balloon floated right over my swimming pool, sending my dogs into a barking frenzy.)

That's why I'm always surprised at how few locals have actually taken to the sky. There are several outfits in town at which to book a flight, so it's as simple as picking a date and a company.

I opted for **Rainbow Ryders.** They've been in business for 40 years, and all their pilots are FAA-certified, have flown more than 50,000 hours, and have a combined 200 years of experience. Plus, their balloons are pretty.

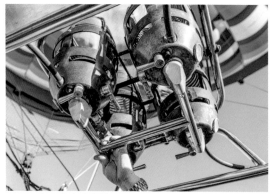

powering a hot-air balloon

soaring over the desert

hot-air balloon

▲ hot-air balloons over Phoenix

My husband and I booked the sunrise flight (from $180/person). We met the pilot and our fellow basket-mates at the Rainbow Ryders office about 30 minutes before sunrise. We boarded a shuttle to the launch site, a day-of location determined by wind conditions, usually in northwest Phoenix.

When we arrived at the launch, it was still dark but the first pink and red hues of sunlight were sliding up from the east. Six or eight other ballooning groups were gathered in the same area, each prepping for takeoff. Big canvases of color—fabric that would swell into balloon shapes as soon as the pilots fired them with air—lay in giant folds across the ground.

We huddled with the other passengers in our group as the pilot readied our vessel. With the balloon inflated, he invited us to climb into the basket one by one. And by climb, I mean, *climb*. You slip your foot in a hole on the side of the basket and then swing your leg over to hop inside.

Once we were safely boarded, the pilot sent a fiery plume up and into the balloon. Our basket gently lifted from the ground and that was it; we were drifting up and away on an air current. It was exhilarating.

Earthbound Fun

To participate in the joy of hot air ballooning from the ground, join 20,000 spectators for the annual **Arizona Balloon Classic** (www.abcfest.com). The festival takes place every January at Goodyear Ballpark (1933 S. Ballpark Way, Goodyear) and features balloon races, tethered rides, food and retail vendors, fireworks, and dozens of illuminated balloons that light up in sync with music.

The thing I remember most about the ride is the silence. Not because our group wasn't chatting—we were, mostly "wow!" and "did you see that?" and "can you believe this?"—but because there was a complete absence of wind. Zero sound of rushing air. We were *in* the wind. We heard only bird songs, the creak of the basket, and the whoosh of the flame that powered our flight.

Sometimes our pilot dipped us low to the earth and I spotted a family of javelina trotting through the creosote. Sometimes he soared us sky-high and I saw the entire city below, grids of streets and squares of lawns inching toward the mountains.

In all directions, the views were breathtaking—mountain peaks and emerald golf courses and desert creatures and white blooms of saguaros and a pickup truck dusting along a dirt road. And though familiar sights, I'd never seen them in quite this way before. A chance to look at your hometown with fresh eyes? Priceless.

Connect with...

④ Tour Taliesin West

⑱ Watch the sun set at South Mountain Park

㉓ Soak up city views at Wrigley Mansion

2 Cheer on *lucha libre*
at Crescent Ballroom

Phoenix Essential• Nightlife • Local Scenes

Why Go: When the masked and costumed *luchadores* leap into the ring, get ready for a wild night of *lucha libre* fun. Cheer on the heroes as they do battle against their dastardly foes.

Where: Crescent Ballroom, 308 N. 2nd Ave., 602/716-2222, https://crescentphx.com

Timing: A typical lucha libre match starts around 8pm and runs 2-3 hours. Arizona-based Rockstar Wrestling Alliance hosts the events at Crescent Ballroom. You can buy tickets ($12 general admission, $20 ringside) at the door, but I recommend purchasing them in advance online as lucha libre matches sell out quickly.

Lucha libre is as much about theatrics as it is about tradition. In Mexico and other Latin American countries, and even in Arizona, the sport—wrestling but with costumes and a dramatic story arc—is cherished as an art form and a cultural touchstone that goes back 100 years.

Lucha libre translates to "free fight" or "freestyle fighting." The superhero-like masked *luchadores* fight in highly choreographed matches that follow *novelas* (soap operas), which carry over from performance to performance. These stories build on rivalries between lucha libre promotions (or leagues, in non-wrestling jargon), as well as between the characters themselves. The continuing storylines also keep audiences coming back for more. You get the high-flying, mat-pounding, knee-throwing athleticism of wrestling combined with broad comedy and an engrossing narrative.

So what's the deal with the masks? A luchador's mask is their most important quality. It elevates them from regular personhood into the god-like being that the audience reveres. In the history of lucha libre, a *mascara contra mascara* fight narrative forces the defeated luchador to remove their mask—an irreparable loss of anonymity and a devastating fall from grace.

Crescent Ballroom in downtown Phoenix

lucha libre masks

One of the most famous luchadores in the sport was the Mexican actor, El Santo. He gained fame in 1942 thanks to Mexican television programming airing his matches several times a week. Throughout his 50-year career, El Santo appeared in dozens of movies and comic books and never, ever removed his mask in public until shortly before his death in 1984.

Today's luchadores abide by the same ethos. Masks never come off, under any circumstances, unless you've been defeated. Rockstar Wrestling Alliance is the local promotion for lucha libre matches at **Crescent Ballroom** (as well as at the Rialto Theatre in Tucson, 318 E. Congress St., 520/740-1000, www.rialtotheatre.com), and when the luchadores arrive in the parking lot for their fights, they emerge from cars and trucks fully masked.

During the fast-paced, action-packed matches at the Crescent, airhorns screech and noisemakers bang as the crowds cheer on the *técnicos* (the colorfully costumed, rule-abiding good guys) and boo the *rudos* (the dark-costumed, tough-talking, grizzled bad guys). Reign-

▲ masks for *luchadores*

Eat Like a *Luchador*

Snacking at lucha libre is almost as vital as watching the action in the ring. Crescent Ballroom's **Cocina 10 Kitchen** keeps things authentic with some of the best Mexican fare around. Order yourself a *michelada* (a chilled, spicy, beer *con* tomato juice cocktail) and *al pastor* tacos on homemade corn tortillas.

ing champ Lord Drako usually makes an appearance to defend his title from the up-and-coming luchadores, and deejays spin *cumbia* and dance music in between the fights.

The luchadores exhibit all sorts of acrobatics—jumping, rolling, spinning, flying, flipping, throwing, body slamming—and while there's no argument as to the scripted nature of the antics, the athleticism of these fighters is real. So is the enthusiasm of the audience. It's impossible not to get caught up in the spectacle, impossible not to buy into the ruse, though you know, of course, it's fake.

It's funny. When you give in to the energy of lucha libre, all that jaded irony and hyper self-awareness that we arm ourselves with—not unlike a luchador mask—falls away and you feel something genuine: unbridled joy.

Connect with...

8 Hear local stories at Arizona Storytellers Project
21 Dive into the blues and R&B music scene
32 Savor Sonoran-style food

Taste the Fry Bread House's namesake dish

Phoenix Essential • Native Cultures • Drink and Dine

Why Go: The Fry Bread House was the first Native-owned restaurant in the country to earn a James Beard award, an accolade for the restaurant's Tohono O'odham fare and also for its mission to create a welcoming space in the community for American Indians.

Where: 4545 N. 7th Ave., www.facebook.com/frybreadhouse

Timing: The restaurant opens mid-morning for breakfast and the lunch rush picks up soon after. Despite how busy the one-room eatery gets, midday is the absolute best time to go to relish the buzz of the lunchtime crowd—a diverse mix of Melrose District locals, Native regulars, and visiting tourists.

Let's be clear. Fry bread is not a traditional Native food. Made with white flour, baking powder, salt, and shortening, the pillowy dough's debut in the cuisine of the American Indians of the Southwest is murky. And thorny.

Navajo Indians—who comprise the Navajo Nation, the largest tribe by population in the United States—trace the origins of fry bread to the U.S. government's forced 300-mile migration from Arizona to New Mexico. Known as the "Long Walk," the deportation consisted of more than 50 marches from 1864 to 1866 that removed the Navajo from their land. It was during this time that the government doled out rations of flour, sugar, salt, and lard. It's believed that the tribe used these ingredients to make what we now know as fry bread.

Another theory for fry bread's arrival in the kitchens of Native people was years later, as a 20th-century dish created when tribes began to cook with more commercial ingredients, such as white flour and sugar.

Whatever its origin, know this: For Native people, fry bread symbolizes both their survival and their colonialism.

The James Beard Foundation acknowledged the complicated legacy of fry bread when it honored **The Fry Bread House** in Phoenix with an "America's Classics" designation in

the famous fry bread taco

American Indian artwork by Bunky Echo-Hawk on the outside of Fry Bread House

2012. The judges lauded the restaurant for its "blissfully delicious specialty" and "quality food that reflects the character of the community."

Opened in 1992 by Cecelia Miller, a member of the Tohono O'odham Nation, The Fry Bread House is a beloved family-run neighborhood staple.

Miller (who passed away in 2020 at the age of 81) learned her hand-stretched fry bread technique from her mother while growing up on Tohono O'odham land in southern Arizona. She left a job in real estate to launch the restaurant, introducing Phoenicians to Indigenous foods and offering a home away from home for Native diners. Miller's hiring practices included a dedication to an all-Native staff, with a soft spot for giving Native women—regardless of tribe—an opportunity at employment. Members of her staff stay for years.

Step inside The Fry Bread House and you're greeted with the mouthwatering aromas of traditional Tohono O'odham cuisine—*chumuth*, spicy *pozole*, chippies and salsa—and the nontraditional namesake dish—fry bread.

I recommend return visits in order to try everything on the menu, but if you do nothing

The Power of Art

Post-meal, head to the side of the building. Spanning edge to edge, roof to pavement, is a powerful mural painted by Native artists Bunky Echo-Hawk and Votan Henriquez. In 2020, the Phoenix Indian Center partnered with the National Congress of American Indians and Illuminative to paint Native-themed "Get Out the Vote" murals around Phoenix.

else, get the fry bread. Rolled out flat and wide, then deep fried for a crispy-on-the-edges-fluffy-in-the-middle consistency, fry bread can be ordered two ways. I like the savory version topped with beef, beans, lettuce, cheese, and a cooling dollop of sour cream. For a sweet option, order it slathered with honey, or smothered in chocolate and butter, or simply sprinkled with powdered sugar.

The original iteration of Miller's restaurant was located on Indian School Road and 8th Street. Today, it's a proud member of the Melrose District on 7th Avenue, where it rubs shoulders with the neighborhood's LGBTQ+-friendly shops, bars, and restaurants.

Connect with...

9 Buy authentic American Indian art

11 Feast on soul food at Mrs. White's Golden Rule Café

14 Learn about Arizona's American Indian heritage at the Heard Museum

Tour Taliesin West

Why Go: The ideal way to avoid the throngs of tourists at famed architect Frank Lloyd Wright's winter home? Join one of the smaller, more intimate summer tours.

Where: 12621 N. Frank Lloyd Wright Blvd., Scottsdale, 602/800-5444, https://franklloydwright.org/taliesin-west

Timing: Taliesin West is open year-round. Because Wright designed the buildings to embody indoor-outdoor living, there's no central AC. Summer tours operate during the (relatively) cool mornings, 9am-11:30am Thursday-Sunday. Tours last 60-90 minutes. It's about a 35-minute drive to Taliesin West from downtown Phoenix.

When you live in metro Phoenix, there's no escaping Frank Lloyd Wright.

There's the Scottsdale street named after the architect, for one. And the illuminated blue spire—all edges and angles and points—that he designed in 1957 and which now looms near the Scottsdale Promenade. How about Grady Gammage Auditorium at Arizona State University, which Wright designed to be acoustically perfect? Those landmarks don't even begin to take into account his legacy, which includes homes and buildings sprinkled throughout the Valley designed by students of Wright, each structure wearing Wright-esque architectural details like badges of honor.

Ask anyone who lives here if they've heard of Frank Lloyd Wright, and they'll nod their heads in the affirmative. Ask if they've ever visited his masterpiece, **Taliesin West,** and you might get a different answer. Maybe something like a sheepish shrug of the shoulders and a response along the lines of: "Not yet, but I've been meaning to."

To us locals, visiting Taliesin West feels like a touristy thing to do. And it is. But Taliesin West is an important architectural gem, not just in Arizona, but in the country.

In 1937, on a mesa in Scottsdale's McDowell Mountains, Frank Lloyd Wright designed a complex of buildings as a winter home and architecture school for his apprentices. He

Frank Lloyd Wright's Taliesin West interior

gift shop at Taliesin West

named it Taliesin West after his Wisconsin house, Taliesin, yet he took inspiration from the surrounding desert.

Wright believed in creating structures that allowed for harmony between humans and the environment. It was an architectural philosophy he pioneered called organic architecture. Taliesin West so embodies this ideal that it's now the headquarters for the esteemed Frank Lloyd Wright Foundation, and it was recently named a UNESCO World Heritage Site.

Taliesin West is a place where people from all over the world come to see Wright's groundbreaking designs in person. So, instead of skipping out on the experience altogether, let's embrace it—albeit in the off-season. Two tours are offered in the tourist-free, blazing heat of summer.

The 60-minute "Guided By Wright Tour" ($40/adults, $19/children ages 6-12, reservations required) is a self-paced audio tour that uses recordings from Wright himself, along with added narration from Taliesin West's tour guides. As you walk under Wright's tilted

▴ one of three theaters at Taliesin West

More Than a Souvenir

Gift shops aren't all kitsch mugs and goofy tees—not the one at Taliesin West anyway. **The Frank Lloyd Wright Store** (summer hours, 9am-1pm Thurs.-Sun.) masquerades as a museum, one where all the art is for sale. Pick up wood model kits of Wright-designed buildings, cocktail glasses etched with Wright's signature triangles and circles, glossy art books, leather-stitched satchels, and home decor.

ceilings, through his low-roofed breezeways, and alongside his cool stone walls, you'll hear the architect discuss the art, poetry, and nature that inspired him throughout his lifetime.

The guide-led "Insights Tour" ($40/adults, $19/children ages 6-12, reservations required) is the signature experience at Taliesin West. On the 60-minute journey, you'll visit Wright's private quarters, drafting studio, living room, music pavilion, and the cabaret theater. The connected spaces—rooms that link to terraces that morph into gardens that merge into pools—and the endless windows showcase Wright's compositional balance of human-made structures and the natural landscape. Note, too, his use of local materials, such as desert rock.

His accolades and achievements aside, Frank Lloyd Wright wasn't all that different from most of us: a Midwesterner just trying to flee the harsh winters for the warm Arizona sun.

Connect with...

- **9** Buy authentic American Indian art
- **15** Explore Phoenix's mid-century modern architecture
- **43** Go wine-tasting

Discover new writers at local bookstores

Local Scenes • Art and Culture • Shopping

Why Go: These stores do more than just peddle books. They foster community, they inspire connection, and they amplify voices that have been historically silenced. They're also, quite simply, great places to find your next weekend read.

Where: Changing Hands Bookstore • Grassrootz Bookstore • Palabras Bilingual Bookstore

Timing: All stores host weekly and monthly events, so check each store's calendar for updates.

I discovered my love for Joan Didion later in life. Thinking back now, it seems crazy that I'd never read a word by the acclaimed writer until I was 34. Didion—the woman who chronicled 1960s counterculture from the trenches, won the National Book Award, and was a finalist for the Pulitzer—never crossed my path until the sudden death of my father.

Muddling through grief, I sought comfort in the thing that had always brought me comfort: books. I may have Googled "mourning, self-help," I can't remember, but I somehow stumbled on *The Year of Magical Thinking*. Didion wrote it in 2004 after the death of her husband and illness of her daughter. It was her treatise on loss, and when I read it, I responded immediately to Didion's unflinching, unsentimental take on sorrow. Her incisive prose cut right through my haze of sadness.

The next thing I did was challenge myself to read only books written by women—my way of making up for the fact that I, a voracious reader, had somehow missed Didion. What else had I missed, I wondered? What other writers were flying under the radar? (Although I fully acknowledge that Didion in no way flies under the radar.)

This led to other literary challenges over the years, like reading only books written by Black women or by American Indian poets. While it may seem limiting to approach books this way, I found the opposite to be true. It cracked my world open, introducing me to writers I'd never encountered before.

Palabras on Roosevelt Street

Changing Hands Bookstore

This is one of the reasons why bookstores that make a special effort to highlight works by underrepresented voices matter. Here are three of my favorites in Phoenix:

Grassrootz (1145 E. Washington St., #200, Phoenix, 480/442-0293, https://grassrootzbookstore.com) is the first and only Black-owned bookstore in Arizona. Owner Ali Nervis lines the shelves with fiction, literature, children's books (many by local Black authors), and titles of historical and social commentary. The latter became especially popular during the COVID-19 pandemic and social justice movements of 2020. "To see the books that people are getting, it shows they're intentionally trying to unlearn and relearn the truth about our history and our society," Nervis told a local newspaper. "As a bookstore, we find ourselves in the position to help educate, and hopefully, bring sustainable change."

First-generation Mexican Rosaura Magaña shares a similar goal. She's the owner of the state's only bilingual bookstore, **Palabras** (906 W. Roosevelt St., Unit 2, Phoenix, 602/595-9600, www.palabrasbookstore.com). She cites watching her parents struggle with language barriers and discrimination as her motivation for wanting to create a space where the local

author reading at Changing Hands

Get to Know...

Shamirrah Hill. She's the Phoenix-based author of the popular children's book The Shy Monster, a beautifully illustrated story about a young Black girl overcoming shyness. Hill and her husband own **DG Self Publishing** (623/396-6305, https://dgselfpublishing.com), a local children's book publishing company that offers creative services—graphic design, illustration—and step-by-step guidance to aspiring BIPOC writers.

Latinx community could feel embraced and represented. The consciously selected collection of books at Palabras showcases authors by, and for, people of color, with an emphasis on Spanish-language offerings. The store has an art gallery; a space for workshops, including a queer writing group by Trans Queer Pueblo; and regularly hosted readings and book clubs.

Though long-running bookstore **Changing Hands** (6428 S. McClintock Dr., Tempe, 480/730-0205, and 300 W. Camelback Rd., Phoenix, 602/274-0067; www.changinghands.com) stocks a broad, mainstream selection of books, they also take care to represent BIPOC stories. The staff-curated reading lists are topical and feature diverse voices; a recent roundup called "The Anti-Racist Reading List" included nearly 50 books by writers both new (Ibram X. Kendi) and classic (Audre Lorde).

Connect with...

- **8** Hear local voices at Arizona Storytellers Project
- **16** Celebrate the Miss Gay Arizona America Pageant
- **22** Shop local

6 Toast an Arizona brew

Drink and Dine • Local Scenes

Why Go: Lots of places serve beer. But these hyper-local breweries pair a well-crafted brew with cultural impact—from leading the way in sustainability efforts to speaking out against social injustice.

Where: Find the breweries at their locations throughout Phoenix.

Timing: These taprooms are open daily, most of them starting at 11am or noon. All offer outdoor beer gardens or patio seating. Crowds peak Friday through Sunday. If you're down for sharing tables with strangers, stop by on the weekend; if you prefer to sip quietly by yourself, visit on a weekday afternoon.

There are thousands of tweets, lengthy articles, even entire books dedicated to telling you exactly what makes a beer great. This is not one of those pieces.

My beer tastes are simple. I like ambers that are malty and IPAs that are hazy. Beyond that, I don't know much about flavor profiles and I'm not the most adventurous beer drinker. What I do find impressive, however, are the people and places who fearlessly shake up the industry. Especially those in our local brew scene.

Like Megan Greenwood. She opened **Greenwood Brewing** (922 N. 5th St., 602/875-8577, https://greenwoodbrews.com) in Phoenix in 2020. Greenwood is one of the state's few female brewers, and her brewery is the city's first one that's entirely female-owned. But it's not just about the superlatives for Greenwood. It's about actionable change. Consider this: When Greenwood Brewing first opened, nearly 95 percent of the job applicants were women, most of whom had never worked in a brewery. That speaks volumes as to what inclusivity can do for empowering people. And, in addition to creating a welcoming space for a female brew staff, Megan Greenwood designed a taproom equally inviting for all guests—upholstered stools in deep green, gold light fixtures, warm woods—and crafted beers that are approachable for first-timers. I'm a fan of the Luna Amber Ale (toasted caramel, round and sweet) and, in a departure from my norm, the crisp and tart blueberry wheat beer.

1: pint at Wren House 2: a collection of beer labels from Wren House 3: Phantasm beer for sale at Arizona Wilderness Brewing 4: Arizona Wilderness Brewing

Leah Huss is another female brewer in the local craft beer community. She co-owns Tempe's popular **Huss Brewing** (100 E. Camelback Rd., #160, 602/441-4677, www.huss-brewing.com) with her husband, and before launching Huss, Leah co-owned and operated the much beloved, now shuttered Papago Brewing in Scottsdale for 14 years. As one of the pioneers of Phoenix's craft brew scene, Leah is a leader in the community. In partnership with the Arizona Craft Brewers Guild, she organized and hosted an all-women brewing event at Huss; nearly 75 women from various aspects of the industry—brewers, managers, sales reps—gathered to create the first official all-female brewed beer in the state. Leah currently runs the business and marketing operations at Huss, expanding it into the third-largest independently owned brewery in Arizona. (My go-to Huss Beer is the Scottsdale Blonde, refreshing with a hint of sweetness.)

Arizona Wilderness Brewing (201 E. Roosevelt St., Phoenix, 480/462-1836, https://azwbeer.com) lives up to its name by employing land and water conservation efforts at every stage of the beer-making process. The brewery supports Arizona farmers by using locally

▲ Arizona Wilderness Brewing in downtown Phoenix

Did You Know?

Arizona's first commercial brewery opened in Tucson in 1864. Owner Alexander Levin overcame obstacles like alkaline water from the Rillito River and unreliable supply chains to successfully operate several breweries for 20 years. But then the railroad arrived, and with it dozens of out-of-state beers that saturated the market and put local breweries out of business.

and regionally grown fruit in nearly all of their beers (juicy watermelons in the gose, for instance, and peaches in the double IPA Peaches & Cream). They partner with other sustainably minded businesses, such as Chandler's Peixoto Coffee, whose locally roasted beans flavor the Superstition Coffee Stout, and Agritopia in Gilbert, which offered up 500 pounds of hand-processed peaches for the sour ale Phantasm. Plus, the brewery's Belgian-style witbier uses very little water and is mashed with Arizona-grown Sonoran white wheat.

Small but mighty **Wren House Brewing** (2125 N. 24th St., 602/244-9184, www.wrenhousebrewing.com) joined Arizona Wilderness (and 19 other regional breweries) to establish the Western Rivers Brewers Council. This organization partners with Audubon Arizona to advocate for sound water policy to benefit rivers, economies, habitats, and birds and other wildlife. Recently, breweries on the council collaborated on bird-themed beers to get the word out about water conservation. Wren House created the Rain Crow, a wheat IPA in honor of the western yellow-billed cuckoo, nicknamed "rain crow." Wren House also crafted a specialty beer called Black Excellence, an imperial stout for which the proceeds of sales were donated to the NAACP.

Connect with...

12 Play hooky at a Cactus League Spring Training game
13 Ply the waters of Tempe Town Lake
20 Lace up your boots for an urban hike on Trail 100

Take a field trip on the Fresh Foodie Trail

Drink and Dine • Local Scenes • Scenic Drives

Why Go: Love food? Fascinated by farms? Then this is the culinary excursion for you. On a day trip, sample and sip, pick and pluck, and tour and taste the year-round bounty growing in Phoenix's East Valley.

Where: Curated by Visit Mesa, the Fresh Foodie Trail charts a course through the towns of Mesa, Queen Creek, and Gilbert. • 480/827-4700; www.visitmesa.com, www.freshfoodietrail.com

Timing: Plan for 6-7 hours to complete the Fresh Foodie Trail (free), which you can do year-round. Check out apples, olives, and pumpkins in the fall (and family-friendly harvest festivals); heirloom wheat and citrus in the winter; and peaches and pears in summer and spring. Plus, chef-hosted cooking classes each month and farmers markets every week.

Just on the outer edges of our sprawling metropolis, somewhere between where the pavement ends and the rugged mountains begin, produce-growing farm fields and fruit-bearing orchards stake their claim.

Phoenix's growing history dates back to the ancient Hohokam people. These skilled farmers built an intricate network of canals—which we still use today—throughout the valley to funnel water to fields where they grew corn, cotton, beans, and squash. Modern family farms on the outskirts of the city carry on the region's rich agricultural heritage. And in the East Valley, you can learn all about it (and nosh on goodies) on the **Fresh Foodie Trail.**

Starting in Mesa, the "trail" (a roundup of East Valley food producers and eateries) takes you to about a dozen agri-destinations, including citrus groves, pumpkin patches, apple orchards, dairy farms, flour mills, wineries, and farm stands.

At **True Garden Urban Farm** (5949 E. University Dr., Mesa, 480/305-8985, https://truegarden.com), see a solar-powered, vertical greenhouse that uses less water, takes up less space, and maintains a smaller carbon footprint than traditional growing spaces. Within the three-square-foot, nine-foot-high tower, farmers can grow 52 greens, herbs, vegetables,

an orchard dinner on the Fresh Foodie Trail

fruits, and flowers. When you visit, ask the owners to show you around, and be sure to shop for seedlings for your own garden or fresh produce from theirs.

Tour **Superstition Dairy Farm** (3440 S. Hawes Rd., Mesa, 602/432-6865, https://superstitionfarmaz.com) to meet the animals producing the butter, milk, eggs, cheese, and ice cream that the family-owned farm is famous for. Don't leave without stocking up on fresh dairy products, plus local jams and honey.

The town of Queen Creek is home to two of the more popular stops on the trail: **Queen Creek Olive Mill** (25062 S. Meridian Rd., Queen Creek, 480/888-9290, www.queencreekolivemill.com), where olives are grown, harvested, pressed, and bottled and visitors are invited to enjoy tastings of the oils, olives, vinegars, and tapenades; and **Schnepf Farms** (24610 S. Rittenhouse Rd., Queen Creek, 480/987-3100, www.schnepffarms.com), a 300-acre, U-pick farm that hosts year-round events such as outdoor dinners, October's Pumpkin & Chili Party, and February's Peach Blossom Festival.

No disrespect to the 1915-planted citrus groves at **B&B Citrus Farms** (3434 N. Val

Agritopia in Gilbert

Hidden Caches and Surprise Treasures

Gear up for a geocaching adventure on the Fresh Foodie Trail. Using a mobile app on your phone or a GPS device, scour the places along the trail for 10 secreted-away stashes as part of the Visit Mesa GeoTour. Download the free app (www.geocaching.com/play/mobile), turn on your location services, and search under GeoTour (GT49A) for the current list of caches.

Vista Dr., Mesa, 480/459-3050, www.bbcitrusfarms.com) or to the stone-milled ancient and heritage grains of one of my favorite places, **Hayden Flour Mills** at Sossaman Farms (22100 S. Sossaman Rd., Queen Creek, 480/557-0031, www.haydenflourmills.com), but the highlight of the Fresh Foodie Trail is arguably Agritopia.

Known as one of the nation's first "agrihoods," the 160-acre, live-work-eat-learn-farm-shop **Agritopia** (3000 E. Ray Rd., Gilbert, 480/563-4745, www.agritopia.com) features a residential community, urban gardens, maker spaces for local artisans, several craft breweries, a collaborative winery, and nationally renowned restaurants, such as Joe's Farm Grill. No matter where you venture on the property, you'll find places—like the farmers market, coffee shop, and café—that showcase the bounty of the region. Look for cheese curds by Arizona Dairymen, meats from The Pork Shop, Agritopia-grown greens, and Arizona honey.

The Fresh Foodie Trail is easily doable as a self-guided journey, but **Detours American West** (866/438-6877, https://detoursamericanwest.com, $185/person) offers a full-day guided tour of the trail with transportation, complimentary tastings, lunch, take-home treats, and behind-the-scenes peeks and educational insights at several of the stops.

Connect with...

- 44 Go wine-tasting
- 50 Wander lavender fields
- 51 Pick saguaro fruit

Hear local voices at Arizona Storytellers Project

Art and Culture • Local Scenes

Why Go: During an evening of listening to friends and neighbors talk about their lives, you might experience moments of transformation, lightning strikes of profundity, a few tears, and a lot of laughter.

Where: Venue locations located throughout metro Phoenix, www.storytellersproject.com

Timing: Storytelling events occur year-round, usually 4-6 per season. Each event runs about 90 minutes and comprises 6-8 storytellers. General admission is free, although attendees are welcome to offer their support via a $3 Conscientious Support ticket or an annual membership of $35 or $100, which includes perks, merch, and access to members-only conversations.

I can admit it. I'm no storyteller. I can spin a funny anecdote or two, like about the time I tried to water ski after a tequila-soaked day on the beach, or when my dog unlocked the gate by himself to trot around the neighborhood.

But to parse through the transformational impact an experience had on me? Well, that could take a lifetime. So I have a deep appreciation for those who can do it in 6-10 minutes, and in a room full of strangers, no less. I'm referring to storytelling. As in oral storytelling, where people stand in front of an audience and talk about the pivotal experiences that changed their lives. In our home state, this manifests as the **Arizona Storytellers Project,** part of the USA TODAY Network.

Founded by *Arizona Republic* journalist Megan Finnerty in 2011, the Storytellers Project grew from a handful of small events at local restaurants to a nationwide series of live storytelling nights at major venues in more than 20 U.S. cities. (Here in Phoenix, venues have included the Desert Botanical Garden, Phoenix Art Museum, and the Scottsdale Center for the Performing Arts.) The project's mission: "Creating empathy and understanding across America."

Every Storytellers Project night focuses on a theme, and storytellers receive profession-

Kanu Masenda Jacobsen

Erick Cedeno

Marilee Lasch

Arizona Storytellers Project

al coaching before the event. Storytellers can be anyone: authors, teachers, military veterans, entrepreneurs, engineers, athletes, mothers, sons, your neighbor, a friend. Each storyteller details a first-person story—in 10 minutes or less—on theme-related topics like food, work, the outdoors, families, race, gender identity, love, life, death.

Angelica Lindsey-Ali, a Muslim educator, once talked about not quite fitting in when she first moved to Phoenix from Detroit.

Joanna de'Shay, the daughter of a Nigerian father and Russian mother who identifies as a Black Russian, discussed how she found design inspiration for her Phoenix-based fashion line from the women she admired while growing up in Ghana.

And Jan Wichayanuparp recalled childhood visits to Thailand to see her grandmother, and how her very favorite part of the trip was the food—a likely indicator of Wichayanuparp's future success as co-founder of the award-winning Sweet Republic Ice Cream.

Other Storytellers Project events featured 14-year-old Jack Florez, who shared his story of living with cerebral palsy; Joy Young, a poet who talked about coming out to their family

Your Turn

You can go from audience member to storyteller like *that*. The Arizona Storytellers Project invites people of all ages, backgrounds, and experience levels to take the stage. Sign up online (www.storytellersproject.com/tell), work with the project's coordinators to craft your story into a tidy narrative, and receive coaching and guidance for the big performance.

after the death of their grandmother; and Millie Hollandback, whose life as a young girl was shaped by her role as the interpreter for her deaf parents.

The stories can be funny, surprising, wild, tender, grief-filled and hope-filled, heartwarming or heartbreaking. But the stories are always true. And they're always underscored by astute insights into how it is we humans make our way through this world—sometimes fumbling, usually stumbling, but every now and then finding moments of grace and beauty when we least expect it.

Connect with...

5 Discover new writers at local bookstores

11 Feast on soul food at Mrs. White's Golden Rule Café

14 Learn about Arizona's American Indian heritage at the Heard Museum

Buy authentic American Indian art

Native Cultures • Art and Culture • Shopping

Why Go: Buy Indigenous art from the hands of the people who create it. Not only does this financially benefit Arizona's Native community, but it gives shoppers a chance to connect more meaningfully with Native stories.

Where: Storefront located at 7125 E. Main St., Scottsdale • outdoor market at 9151 E. Indian Bend Rd., Scottsdale, 707/733-6443, www.nativeartmarket.org

Timing: The Native Art Market's storefront is open daily 9am-7pm. The outdoor market runs from November 1 to April 1. Hours are 9am-4pm Saturday-Sunday. The storefront location offers more convenient hours, but if you'd like to meet the artists directly, I recommend planning a Saturday or Sunday visit to the outdoor seasonal market. Set aside 2-4 hours to browse.

Whether it's food or clothing, the origins of what we consume and buy aren't always clear. That's not true when you purchase something at the **Native Art Market.**

As the first Native-owned store in Scottsdale, the shop serves as a platform for American Indian artists and artisans. Nearly 200 Native businesses stock their goods at Native Art Market; everything is handmade (no imports or imitations), and product sales go back to the Indigenous business owners and artists.

The obvious mission of the market is to let shoppers buy art, clothing, jewelry, and more directly from the people who make the goods, eliminating the often costly go-between and thwarting efforts by overseas sellers to imitate—and mass produce—Native works.

The less obvious mission, and the one that resonates most profoundly for owner Heather Tracy, is giving American Indian artisans the chance to present their works and, as she says, "correct our cultural stories." Economic empowerment meets cultural awareness.

Tracy and her mother, Denise Rosales, are members of the Navajo Nation. Their family has been sculpting pottery and weaving rugs and making jewelry for five generations. Though they sell their crafts at festivals and art walks, Tracy and Rosales sought a year-round solution for artists to showcase their goods. So they launched Native Art Market in

Native Art Market in Old Town Scottsdale

2018, first as an outdoor venue and then, in 2020, as a brick-and-mortar storefront in Old Town Scottsdale.

The outdoor market features 40 artists who meet with shoppers every weekend to share their story, talk about their process, and discuss their art. The market supports 400 Native families and represents members from Arizona's 22 tribes.

Combining the successes of the outdoor market and the storefront, Native Art Market has generated more than $250,000 in funding for American Indian businesses and artisans.

Wondering what to do on a visit to the Native Art Market? Peruse the drawings from Kyle Nash. See beaded jewelry by Kynard Begay. Admire the handmade flutes from Melvin Shorty. Or try on serape sandals with custom stitching by Tina Yazzie.

Enjoy weekly live performances such as flute playing and hoop dancing. Take part in "Sip-n-Shops," which invite you to browse with a glass of wine or a cup of coffee.

And definitely take the time to talk to the artists. Ask them what tribe they're from,

▲ candles for sale

Diversify Your Playlist

For analog music fans, a prime spot to shop is **Drumbeat Indian Arts** (4143 N. 16th St., Phoenix, 602/266-4823, https://drumbeatindianarts.com, 10am-4pm Tues.-Sat.). In business for more than 30 years, Drumbeat is the largest wholesale and retail source for authentic traditional and contemporary American Indian music. The store stocks selections from 50 recording labels, including locally owned Canyon Records, as well as independent releases from native artists like Keith Secola and Floyd Red Crow.

how long they've been mastering their craft, and from whom they learned. Inquire about the artistic process, the materials used, and the symbolism in the finished product.

These artists and artisans have stories to tell. Go ahead and listen.

Connect with...

3 Taste the Fry Bread House's namesake dish

5 Discover new writers at local bookstores

14 Learn about Arizona's American Indian heritage at the Heard Museum

10 Stretch out at goat yoga

Phoenix Essential • Fun for Families and Kids

Why Go: Goat yoga may be a "thing" now, but Arizona Goat Yoga is supposedly the place that started it all. Relax with cute, cuddly goats and meet the two women who helped launch a national craze.

Where: Welcome Home Ranch, 26601 S. Val Vista Dr., Gilbert, 480/269-4144, https://goatyoga.com

Timing: Goat yoga classes ($15/person in advance, $20/person for drop-in) are held outdoors year-round, even in summer. Classes last an hour, although you can certainly stay longer to pet the goats and take pictures. Start times vary depending on season and weather. Arizona Goat Yoga releases a class schedule on the 15th of every month, so check dates and times before reserving your spot.

Yoga with goats? It makes no sense, really. Yoga provides all sorts of mental, emotional, and physical health benefits on its own. Having a goat climb on your back and canoodle your neck seems like it would be more distraction than added boon. And yet pairing the two together has spawned a nationwide trend that people—yogis and non-yogis alike—can't seem to get enough of.

Here's how it works: A yoga instructor leads a class through a session while goats mill about, interacting with their human counterparts. The animals nuzzle and nibble and climb and perch on the yogis as they roll into stretches like Downward-Facing Dog, Plank, and Bridge. Goats' natural inclination is to climb—no coaxing or cajoling necessary to get them up, on, and over your body. Goats are intelligent, too, and gentle in nature, so there's nothing to fear about the close encounters.

Though there's some argument as to who was the first to conceive of the idea, it appears likely that Arizona natives April Gould and Sarah Williams, who started **Arizona Goat Yoga** in Gilbert, were among the first. Their goat yoga business predates that of Oregonian Lainey Morse by a year, though Morse so steadfastly believes in her first-to-find claim that she trademarked her company's name as Original Goat Yoga.

The owners of Arizona Goat Yoga love other animals, too.

yoga class

In early 2015, Gould, a retired professional water-skier, was training for the televised athletic competition *American Ninja Warrior* when she started using her farm goats as training partners. She invited them to hop onto her back as additional weight while she exercised (the television show even coined her the "Goat Whisperer"). Williams, a certified yoga instructor and also a former *American Ninja Warrior* competitor, started a business around the same time that combined yoga with props. In the summer, she did yoga on paddleboards. In winter, she found inspiration in her friend Gould's farm goats. Goat yoga was officially born, at least in Arizona.

What's more important than who was first—the team of Gould and Williams, or Morse—is the fact that goat yoga is *fun*.

Arizona Goat Yoga classes are held outside on the grounds of the farm, and class sizes can be as large as 100 people. Attendees span all ages and fitness levels, but the one requirement is that you're comfortable with animals. In addition to the goats, the farm is also home

For the Record

Arizona Goat Yoga achieved a Guinness World Record in February 2019 for hosting the largest goat yoga class. They rounded up 351 people and 84 goats inside Mesa Amphitheatre to set the record. Six months later, this was shattered when Grady Goat Foundation in Florida held a goat yoga class of 501 people.

to horses, cows, chickens, and alpacas, although the yoga classes take place in an enclosed area.

You can snap as many photos as you'd like, and you're even welcome to pick up the goats and hold them for some fuzzy hugs. The babies will likely fall asleep in your arms, so if you're serious about maintaining your Warrior II pose, wait until class is over to snuggle.

Bring your own mat and dress comfortably. Oh, and don't worry about the goat poo. The animals will "go" around you. Just sweep away the pellets and say *namaste*.

Connect with...

7 Take a field trip on the Fresh Foodie Trail
12 Play hooky at a Cactus League Spring Training game
36 See wild horses on the Salt River

11

Feast on soul food at Mrs. White's Golden Rule Café

Drink and Dine • Local Scenes

Why Go: Mrs. White's serves what is arguably the best fried chicken in the state. If that's not reason enough to visit, how about the fact that it's been open for nearly 60 years, which is downright historic in a young city like Phoenix.

Where: 808 E. Jefferson St., 602/262-9256, http://mrswhitesgoldenrulecafe.com

Timing: The restaurant is open daily from mid-morning until early evening. Go for lunch if you're in the mood for the lively hustle and bustle of the midday crowd, but if you want to linger awhile over your black-eyed peas—and chat it up with the regulars—grab a table for an early dinner.

The walls of **Mrs. White's Golden Rule Café** are covered in handwritten messages inked in pen and marker. Some are words of praise from locals for the family-run restaurant's Southern food. Some are daily specials scrawled in large block letters: "Fridays Only Okra Gumbo." Others are notes left by customers, proof that someone, at some time, had been there.

Also on the walls (and lining the lunch counter and hanging over the wooden booths and stacked by the cash register) are framed culinary awards, newspaper clippings hailing the restaurant, and family photos, including those of the owner and restaurant's namesake, Elizabeth White.

White turned 98 in 2021 and still owns and operates the popular eatery in downtown Phoenix. If you think that's an impressive feat, consider this: The Black American opened Mrs. White's Golden Rule Café in 1964, when Phoenix was still a segregated city.

Born in 1923, White left Texas for Phoenix to help her brother run his restaurant, the Church Café. It was situated, you guessed it, in a church. She says they drove all night from Texas on New Year's Day 1963, arriving in Arizona on the second day of the year.

When her brother decided to move to Georgia, White opened the Golden Rule as a means of supporting herself and her children. The origin of the restaurant's name? White

Mrs. White's serves chicken fried steak every day of the week.

never handed bills to the clientele; instead, she relied on the honor system for customers to tell her what they ate and how much they owed.

As most of us who live in Arizona know, authentic Southern fare is hard to come by, even today. In 1964, however, Mrs. White's was the only soul food joint in town. Her restaurant quickly became a gathering spot for the 1960s-era Black community in Phoenix.

Her menu offered Southern classics, such as smothered pork chops, chicken fried steak, catfish, and, of course, her famous fried chicken—as coveted and desired today as it was 60 years ago. Sides included cabbage, red beans, and macaroni and cheese; drinks ranged from Kool-Aid and lemonade to iced tea and milk. For dessert: timeless cobblers and homemade cakes.

The restaurant's menu remains largely unchanged, a fact to which White attributes her success for the better part of a century. As she once told a newspaper reporter: "I believe in being faithful and consistent with everything. You can't come in here one day, one way, and have something different from what it was yesterday. It has to be consistent."

Mrs. White's has been a favorite eatery for soul food lovers since 1964.

A Family Affair

If the name Larry White sounds familiar, that's because the owner of the wildly successful restaurant chain **Lo-Lo's Chicken and Waffles** (locations throughout metro Phoenix and in Nevada and Texas, https://loloschickenandwaffles.com) is the grandson of Elizabeth White. His first restaurant gig was bussing tables at Mrs. White's Golden Rule Café. From there, he began to perfect his fried chicken recipe for which Lo-Lo's is now famous.

That reliability—in both the food and the space itself, which wears its lived-in feel well—extends to White's hospitality, too. She's endured a lot, from Jim Crow and Civil Rights struggles to the current Black Lives Matter movement and COVID-19 pandemic. But she never wavers. She makes sure her restaurant still acts as a welcoming place for the city's Black community, serving up home-cooked food in a room covered, quite literally, in messages from the past and present.

Connect with...

5 Discover new writers at local bookstores

17 Go behind the scenes at sports stadiums

21 Dive into the blues and R&B music scene

12 Play hooky at a Cactus League Spring Training game

Fun for Families and Kids

Why Go: Phoenicians live for the glorious spring months of February and March. And why not? Clear skies, warm sun, cool breezes, and 30 straight days of America's favorite pastime.

Where: Stadiums in Glendale, Mesa, Peoria, Phoenix, Scottsdale, Surprise, and Tempe • 877/636-2783, https://cactusleague.com

Timing: Major League Baseball's spring training kicks off at the end of February and runs through March. There are seven games per day played at 10 stadiums throughout the Phoenix metro area. Day games start around 1pm; evening games start at 6pm or 7pm.

Even before the first pitch is thrown, it's easy to spot the early signs of spring training season in Phoenix: an uptick in vehicles with California and Colorado license plates, longer waits at restaurants, and an inordinate amount of Chicago Cubs attire. As soon as you get that first afternoon out-of-office reply from a co-worker, you know **Cactus League Spring Training** is in full swing (ha!).

In its simplest definition, Major League Baseball (MLB) spring training is a series of exhibition games between professional teams before the regular season commences. It's a chance for new players to test out their chops and established ones to warm up.

In Arizona, Tucson used to host 2 of the 15 teams that travel here annually for pre-season games. (The other 15 MLB teams play in Florida's Grapefruit League.) But now metro Phoenix hosts all 15, making it much more convenient to duck out of the office for a day in the sunshine.

Not into baseball? Doesn't matter. The joy of spring training is there's something for everyone. For die-hard fans, it's a rare chance to see veteran players and up-and-comers in intimate settings as each Cactus League stadium is small and cozy, with seats close to the action (tickets from $45). For families with energetic little ones and laid-back folks who like to

Meet up with friends at a Cactus League Spring Training game.

Chicago Cubs

Tempe Diablo Stadium

▲ relaxed outfield viewing at Salt River Fields

▲ Cactus League Spring Training action

Origin Story

Before the 1940s, most MLB teams attended spring training in Florida. But in 1945, Bill Veeck, the owner of the Milwaukee Brewers' Triple-A team, witnessed firsthand the racism of Jim Crow-era Florida and sold the team to move to his ranch in Tucson. He couldn't stay away from baseball for long, though. In 1947, he purchased the Cleveland Indians. After signing the American League's first Black American player—Larry Doby—to the team, Veeck brought the Indians to Arizona to train.

lounge, the grassy lawns overlooking the outfields (tickets from $25) are perfect on a sunny day. Even foodies will enjoy an afternoon at the ballpark—from traditional baseball fare like hot dogs and shelled peanuts to chef-crafted cuisine and local brews, Cactus League Spring Training doesn't skimp on good eats.

Stadiums are all over the Valley, so it's easy to pop into one wherever you are, especially since teams go head to head every day all day. I favor games at Salt River Fields because a) it has killer views of the McDowell Mountains, and b) I've got to support our Arizona Diamondbacks. Each stadium is distinctive, though, so make time to check out as many as possible.

Connect with...

6 Toast an Arizona brew
17 Go behind the scenes at sports stadiums
22 Shop local

13 Ply the waters of Tempe Town Lake

Phoenix Essential • Outdoor Adventures

Why Go: There's no better way to spend a sunny day than drifting along the waves of this urban lake, with Tempe's skyscrapers lining its southern edge and the red buttes of Papago Park rising to the north.

Where: 620 N. Mill Ave., Tempe, 480/355-6060, www.downtowntempe.com/go/tempe-town-lake

Timing: Consider a half day of recreation at Tempe Town Lake. If the temperatures are warm, arrive in the morning to take advantage of SUP yoga or to rent one of the pedal boats, then break for lunch at a Tempe eatery on Mill Avenue. To catch sunset, arrive midday to stretch your legs on the lakeside trails or picnic on the lawn, then "put in" sometime in the late afternoon.

There was a time when Tempe Town Lake was a dry, dusty shell. Scrub brush broke through hard cracks in the dirt and lizards scurried up embankments. If you think I'm describing a scene from hundreds of years ago, think again. In 1998, I was a college freshman at Arizona State University. On an early-morning jog along Mill Avenue, I stumbled on this giant crater in the earth. I scurried down the steep side—lizard-style—to reach the empty lake bed, and then I ran east into the sunrise. This turned out to be one of my favorite runs for all of six months. Then the City of Tempe began work on what would become one of the prettiest recreation spots in the metro area.

Today, Tempe Town Lake flows for two miles, going west from McClintock Road and east to Priest Road. A portion of the Salt River was dammed and more water was added to create the lake. Greenbelts, grassy lawns, and hilly knolls line the lake's edge on the north and south sides, and a pedestrian-only bridge connects the two. On any given morning, you might see crew teams slicing through the waves or an angler casting a line. SUP yoga classes might be drifting in the middle of the sparkling water. By mid-afternoon, you'll see couples in pedal boats and people in kayaks and canoes. And at all hours, earbud-clad joggers, walkers with dogs, and cyclists traverse the paved paths.

 brews at the Shop Beer Co. near Tempe Town Lake

Fourth of July at Tempe Town Lake

Tempe Town Lake

A Meeting Place

Tempe Town Lake is the unofficial event capital of the Valley. The swim portions of several triathlons take place here, including Ironman Arizona, as well as music festivals, beer and wine tastings, the holiday-themed Fantasy of Lights Boat Parade, and Arizona's largest Fourth of July celebration.

My favorite way to play at Tempe Town Lake is to bring my kayak (permits required, available online, $10 per boat per day) mid-morning and spend a few hours paddling around. The best spot to put in is on the north side of the lake. There's a parking lot close to the water and a sandy bank that makes it easy to walk in a boat. Head to the east side of the lake first; it's less crowded and there are little nooks to explore. If the sun's blazing, take shade breaks underneath the Mill Avenue Bridge. If you don't have your own vessel, you can **rent boats on-site:** kayaks, electric boats, paddleboards, and pedal boats.

kayaking Tempe Town Lake

Conclude the afternoon with brews at **The Shop Beer Co.,** on the south side. It's dog-friendly (major plus!), offers a breezy outdoor patio, and the beers are great. I order Reflections of Society in Literature because I like the name.

For such a big city, metro Phoenix's outdoor activities are truly rugged, but what I love about Tempe Town Lake is how decidedly *urban* it is. Not everyone is a fan of Tempe's recent slate of high-rise condos and glass-walled buildings that have gone up on the lake's south side, but I think the shiny windows and sharp angles lend a cosmopolitan feel. And at sunset, the reds and pinks and oranges reflect off the skyscrapers and ripple across the water, making this one of the best places to be at dusk.

Connect with...

6 Toast an Arizona brew

7 Take a field trip on the Fresh Foodie Trail

12 Play hooky at a Cactus League Spring Training game

14 Learn about Arizona's American Indian heritage

at the Heard Museum

Native Cultures • Phoenix Essential • Art and Culture

Why Go: Few museums surpass the Heard Museum when it comes to showcasing American Indian art, advancing American Indian artists, and presenting the American Indian experience—past and present—within the larger cultural context of our country.

Where: 2301 N. Central Ave., Phoenix, 602/252-8840, https://heard.org

Timing: The museum is open year-round, Tuesday through Sunday. Admission costs $20 for adults, $17 seniors, $9 students and children ages 6-17, and is free for children ages younger than 6 and for American Indian tribe members. To save $3 on adult and senior admission fees, you can purchase tickets online. Admission is free for everyone on the first Friday of the month. Set aside a half day to tour the museum and another hour to shop the goods in the gift store or grab a bite to eat at the café.

Pablita Velarde was one of the most accomplished painters of the 20th century—a woman in a male-dominated art form, an American Indian in a white world. The New Mexico-born Pueblo artist depicted traditional lifeways that she feared would be lost, using her expressive art to share her people's stories.

Iva Honyestewa, from Second Mesa, Arizona, weaves baskets in traditional Hopi styles: *poota* (coil) and *tutsaya* (sifter). She's been weaving since she was young, learning the methods from her cousin. Iva gained notoriety for creating the *pootsaya*, a new Hopi basket that Iva is the only one in the world weaving.

An example of contemporary Diné, artist Raven Chacon's mesmerizing work includes *Still Life No. 3*. The multimedia art installation blends sound, light, and text in a 24-hour cycle that retells the *Diné Bahane'*, the Navajo origin story of emergence.

Pablita Velarde. Iva Honyestewa. Raven Chacon. These are just three names among the hundreds of American Indian artists whose stories come to vivid life within the walls of the **Heard Museum.**

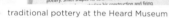

RICHARD ZANE SMITH
Wyandot, b. 1955
Jar, 2006
Ceramic, pigment

The first piece that the 28-year-old artist entered in the
juried competition at the Heard Museum Guild Indian
Fair & Market in 1983 won first place in traditional
pottery. Smith shapes his ceramics from thin coils of clay.

traditional pottery at the Heard Museum

American Indian performance

hoop dancing

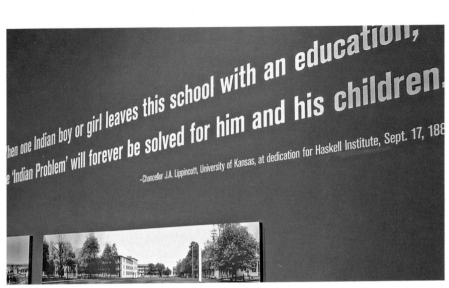

When one Indian boy or girl leaves this school with an education, the 'Indian Problem' will forever be solved for him and his children.

—Chancellor J.A. Lippincott, University of Kansas, at dedication for Haskell Institute, Sept. 17, 188

Heard Museum

Founded in 1929, the Heard presents the art of American Indians, collaborating with the artists and tribal communities to offer first-person perspectives of their lives and cultures. The museum's collection of 4,000 works features art from the 20th century to today and includes creations by some of the best historic and modern American Indian artists.

The museum's permanent exhibits walk you through the traditions, art, and lifeways of Arizona's 22 American Indian tribes, as well as that of the region's ancient cultures like the Hohokam people, who vanished sometime between 1350 and 1450. Key collections include Hopi *katsina* dolls, Navajo textiles and jewelry, Zuni jewelry, and Southwestern ceramics and baskets.

Rotating exhibits and year-round shows feature the art of American Indians outside of Arizona as well, sometimes even touching on non-Native artists who were influenced by American Indian culture. I'll never forget an Henri Matisse exhibit that explored the renowned French artist's little-known connection to the Inuit people, and the shared creative impulses between the two.

Save the Date

In February, the top American Indian and Canadian First Nations hoop dancers come together to compete in the prestigious Hoop Dance World Championship, held at the Heard Museum. The competition is open to the public. The following month, the Heard hosts the Indian Fair & Market, an acclaimed event that draws 15,000 visitors who browse the artworks of 600 of the nation's most outstanding American Indian artists.

In addition to the Heard's impressive art collection is the museum's unflinching look at the history of American Indians in the United States.

In the exhibit *Away From Home*, archival material, powerful first-person interviews, works of art, and short films examine the period of U.S. history (beginning in the 1870s) when the government tried to assimilate American Indians into society by placing them in government-operated boarding schools. Children were taken from families and transported to faraway schools where all elements of their culture, language, and traditions were stripped from them. Generations of children attended these schools before the efforts of advocacy groups, including that of former and current students, succeeded in reforming or closing the schools.

There's much to love about living in Arizona—and much to owe to our state's original inhabitants. The Heard Museum offers a profound way for all of us to feel connected to those who came before, and to one another today.

Connect with...

3 Taste the Fry Bread House's namesake dish
5 Discover new writers at local bookstores
9 Buy authentic American Indian art

15 Explore Phoenix's mid-century modern architecture

Phoenix Essential • Neighborhoods and City Streets • Art and Culture

Why Go: Phoenix has some of the best-preserved examples of mid-century architecture in the country. Even if you're not a fan of the modular, low-slung style, it's worth it to tour these historic 'hoods to track the city's architectural lineage.

Where: Mid-century neighborhoods are located in the central corridor, uptown, and Arcadia. • https://modernphoenix.net • alison@modernphoenix.net

Timing: This is a self-guided tour; you can drive these neighborhoods any time of year, any time of day. Please note that homes are privately owned and not open to the public. The exception to this is Modern Phoenix Week (www.modernphoenix-week.com), an annual seven-day event held every March. During this time, many homeowners in the city's notable mid-century neighborhoods offer guided tours (by reservation only, booked through Modern Phoenix) of their houses' interiors and exteriors. In addition to tours, other Modern Phoenix Week offerings include workshops, lectures, and expos—all related to mid-century architectural history and style.

My Phoenix home was built in 1977. It's ranch-y and long and brick. Very '70s. Though it was constructed a decade after 1965, which is often considered the end of mid-century style, it shares architectural hallmarks with that design period: the sunken living room, a beehive fireplace, giant panes of glass looking out at palm trees.

If you squint, my house *seems* mid-century. But it's definitely not, at least according to the general rubric of the style.

Typically, a mid-century home features a single-story, open-concept layout with floor-to-ceiling windows that open the interior spaces to the outdoors. You'll see overhanging eaves of low-pitched roofs that connect to interior ceilings. The minimalist look includes exposed beams, wood-paneled walls, stone fireplaces, and concrete floors.

This home design gained popularity after World War II, mostly for practicality. Soldiers were returning from war; they needed places to live and houses had to be made quickly. En-

See the angles and lines of Ralph Haver's homes.

Modern Manor mid-century treasures

Marlen Grove sits just south of Bethany Home.

ter modular construction. And because Americans were moving out of the cities and into the suburbs, they had more land so homes could be built out rather than up.

During the 1940s, '50s, and '60s, some of the most influential architects advancing mid-century style worked in California and Arizona, primarily Phoenix. To grasp the scope of their post-war design on Phoenix's growth—and to see the homes and buildings for yourself—visit **Modern Phoenix** (www.modernphoenix.net). Run by architectural expert and historian Alison King, this fact-filled online compendium details all things mid-century, from the must-tour neighborhoods in Phoenix to in-depth profiles of the architects whose vision literally built our city. Here's where to go for angled roofs and breezeblocks galore.

Marion Estates (North of Camelback Road, off 44th Street, between Stanford and McDonald Drives), developed in 1952, is a subdivision that unfolded on the hillsides of Paradise Valley years before the city sprawled north. The two- and three-bedroom homes—now a mix of classic mid-century and more modern renovations—were custom or semi-custom by architects such as Blaine Drake (a contemporary of Frank Lloyd Wright), Al Beadle, and Ralph

⌃ desert landscaping in Paradise Gardens

Where to Shop

If you're dying to outfit your living room with an Eames chair or an oversized lamp shellacked in pea green, then head to **Modern Manor** (4130 N. 7th Ave., Phoenix, 602/266-3376, www.modernmanorphx.com, 11am-6pm daily). The showroom specializes in furniture and decor from the 1940s through the 1980s, every piece hand-sourced, carefully refinished, and meticulously reupholstered to its former glory.

Haver. When taken as a whole, the homes have less uniformity than other neighborhoods, and make for a more interesting scenic drive.

Marlen Grove (from Bethany Home to Montebello Roads, between 10th and 11th Streets) was also established in 1952. The Marlen Grove neighborhood was a citrus-orchard-turned-tract-experiment by architect Ralph Haver. His design touches included angled carport posts, low-angled roofs, glass gables, and clerestory windows—features that have since made this "Haver Hood" one of the most desirable mid-century streetscapes in Phoenix.

Paradise Gardens (from Mountain View Road to Gold Dust Avenue, between 32nd and 36th Streets): Al Beadle designed most of this development in the 1960s, and his futuristic style can be seen all over. The homes are square with flat roofs (although a few have pitched angles), deep overhangs, offset carports, breezeblock fronting the main door, and spiky succulents landscaping the yard. A U-shaped floor plan denotes the Saguaro Model, while the Ocotillo Model showcases a large window wall.

Connect with...

④ Tour Taliesin West
㉒ Shop local
㉓ Soak up city views at Wrigley Mansion

16 Celebrate the Miss Gay Arizona America Pageant

Phoenix Essential • Art and Culture • Local Scenes

Why Go: Show your love for the very best of Arizona's drag queens, who compete for a chance to move on—and possibly win the national crown—at the Miss Gay Arizona America Pageant.

Where: Phoenix-area Pageant locations change annually • 520/275-1824, www.missgayarizonaamerica.com

Timing: The state-level competition of Miss Gay America takes place annually at a venue in metro Phoenix. (Dates and locations change each year; past locations included Aura and Tempe Center for the Arts.) The show starts at 6pm. Because tickets ($25 per person) are general admission and the event is popular, plan to arrive early to secure good seats.

When Espressa Grandé makes her entrance, you know it.

With sky-high heels and even higher hair, Espressa commands the stage every week at her packed show "Thank Grandé It's Friday" at **The Rock** (4129 N. 7th Ave., Phoenix, 602/248-8559, https://therockdmphoenix.com, $3 cover). She puts on an eclectic performance, one that showcases her talents through spoken word and comedy as well as gut-wrenching ballads that can bring the audience to their knees. She doesn't shy away from the tough stuff either, sharing her real-life struggles and opening up discussions on everything from voting to human rights.

One evening with Espressa and it's easy to see why she was crowned the 2019/2020 **Miss Gay Arizona America,** a title that earned her the honor of representing Arizona at the Miss Gay America Pageant.

Established in 1972 and renowned as the oldest, largest, and most prestigious drag queen pageant, Miss Gay America follows a similar format as Miss America, with contestants competing in four categories: male interview, evening gown, talent, and on-stage question.

The talent portion showcases a contestant's ability to entertain; the evening gown category displays their elegance, poise, and glamour; the on-stage question lets a contestant

on stage with Miss Gay Arizona America Pageant contestants

crowning a winner at Miss Gay Arizona America

interact with the audience; and the male interview highlights the male persona as each contestant is interviewed in traditional menswear.

The key to Miss Gay America is that contestants must lean on their creativity and talent to successfully manifest the illusion of being female—no body augmentation allowed. Drag queens use breast and hip pads, wigs, hairstyles, make-up, and flattering outfits to whip up a winning combination that they hope will score them high enough to secure the crown.

There are nearly 30 state and regional preliminary pageants that feed into Miss Gay America. Daniel Eckstrom, whose day job is as the assistant to the dean of Arizona State University's College of Health Solutions, has been the local promoter for Miss Gay Arizona America for more than 15 years. He's a tireless advocate for Phoenix's LGBTQ+ community, and was named Mister Phoenix Pride 2018, a role that helped him raise nearly $50,000 for the Phoenix Pride Scholarship Program.

Charitable donations are also an important aspect of Miss Gay Arizona America; as part

pageant winners

Drag in Phoenix

Beyond the Miss Gay Arizona America Pageant, you can find premier drag shows nearly every night of the week in metro Phoenix. A few not to miss: "Elements After Dark" on Friday at **BS West** (7125 E. 5th Ave., Scottsdale, 480/945-9028, www.bswest.com), "The Robin Banks Show" on Saturday at **Cruisin' 7th** (3702 N. 7th St., Phoenix, 602/212-9888, http://cruisin7th.com), and "Sunday Funday" at **Charlie's** (727 W. Camelback Rd., Phoenix, 602/265-0224, www.charliesphoenix.com). Charlie's is also a supporter and fund-raiser for the Arizona Gay Rodeo Association.

of the Miss Gay America Excellence Foundation, the pageant provides funds to a scholarship for an LGBTQ+-identified community member.

But more than the big hair, more than the glittery evening gowns, more than even the giveback component, Miss Gay Arizona America is an evening when all can belong. Espressa Grandé summed it up best when she interviewed by the *Arizona Republic* after her win:

"In Phoenix, we're fortunate enough to have more LGBTQ+ bars than you might find in other cities, most of which offer a platform for the art of drag. These stages offer opportunities for performers to get in front of an audience and perfect their craft, and they also serve as venues for folks from all walks of life to access this form of creative expression. As drag grows in mainstream popularity, it's important to remember that we're doing this for anyone who enjoys it. Everyone is welcome."

Connect with...

8 Hear local voices at Arizona Storytellers Project
22 Shop local

17 Go behind the scenes at sports stadiums

Fun for Families and Kids

Why Go: What's more thrilling than game-day action? A guided tour of Arizona's professional sports stadiums, where you can visit the secret spots and off-limits-to-the-public areas used by athletes and coaches.

Where: Visit Chase Field in Phoenix and State Farm Stadium in Glendale.

Timing: Tours of Major League Baseball's (MLB) Chase Field are offered Fridays year-round (except on game days). Tours run 90 minutes and tickets cost $7 for adults, $5 for seniors, $3 for children ages 4-6, and are free for children under 3. The 90-minute tours of National Football League's (NFL) State Farm Stadium also run year-round, Wednesday-Saturday (no tours on game days). Tickets cost $9 for adults, $7 for seniors and children ages 4-12, and are free for children under 3.

Arizona may be a young state, but it didn't waste time securing a full roster of professional sports teams. In fact, Phoenix is one of only 13 cities in the country to boast teams in all major sports. That doesn't even include our recent addition of Major League Soccer's Phoenix Rising.

This means that no matter the time of year, sports fans are sure to find a local team to root for. And during those rare times devoid of live sports, you can still feel like part of the action with a behind-the-scenes stadium tour.

Two of Arizona's teams open their doors for guided tours: The NFL's Arizona Cardinals invite guests to explore State Farm Stadium in Glendale, and the MLB's Arizona Diamondbacks welcome visitors to discover the nooks and crannies of Chase Field in downtown Phoenix.

The 1.7-million-square-foot **State Farm Stadium** (1 Cardinals Dr., Glendale, 623/433-7101, www.statefarmstadium.com/stadium-tours/tour) opened in 2006 to much fanfare thanks to a sophisticated design featuring the first retractable natural-grass playing surface in North America and the first retractable inclined roof. The stadium has hosted two NFL

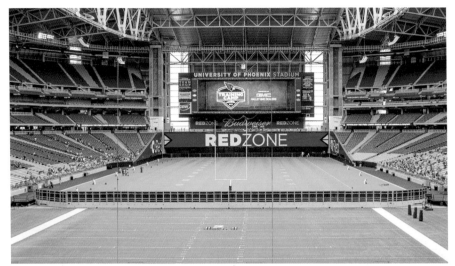

inside Arizona Cardinals' State Farm Stadium

outside Arizona Cardinals' State Farm Stadium

Super Bowl Championships, two National College Football Championships, and one NCAA Final Four Basketball Championship.

During a tour of the stadium, your guide will escort you to all sorts of behind-the-scenes areas, such as the locker room for visiting teams, the television and radio broadcast facilities in the Press Box, the Cardinals Hall of Fame (great for photo ops), the Fan Walls, and the impressive view from the stadium field.

You'll also learn fun facts including how many people the stadium holds, how many people it holds when expanded, and the unique and surprising architectural details inspired by the surrounding desert.

As anyone who's ever attended a D-Backs baseball game at **Chase Field** (401 E. Jefferson St., Phoenix, 602/462-6799, www.mlb.com/dbacks/ballpark/tours) knows, the question of whether or not the roof will be open is a big deal. So much so that the stadium posts a "roof status" online prior to every home game series. That's because during an evening game, when the weather is perfect and sunset morphs the sky into brilliant color at just the right

retractable roof at Arizona Diamondback's Chase Field

What's in a Name?

When Chase Field opened in 1998, the stadium was named Bank One Ballpark after Bank One. Locals shortened it to BOB, and despite the name-change in 2005 after Bank One merged with JPMorgan Chase, die-hard fans still prefer to use their original term of endearment: "Bob."

moment, an open-roof experience at Chase Field can be downright magical. Especially on Fridays when fireworks explode over the field post-game.

So it makes sense that the Chase Field guided tour shares insights into the retractable roof's engineering: nine million pounds of steel, two 200-horsepower motors, four miles of cables, and the technology of a drawbridge can slide the roof open in less than five minutes.

It's not just the roof that's unique, though. The tour also shows off one of MLB's largest high-definition video scoreboards, the first MLB swimming pool in a stadium—the D-Backs Pool, located in right center field—and the Sandlot, where kids can swing for the fences (sort of) in batting cages. Additionally, you'll tour the Press Box, dugout, and playing field. You might even get a chance to meet the Diamondbacks' mascot Baxter.

Connect with...

6 Toast an Arizona brew

12 Play hooky at a Cactus League Spring Training game

18 Watch the sun set at South Mountain Park

Outdoor Adventures • Beautiful Views

Why Go: Where in the center of a major metropolis can you find more than 16,000 acres of wild land, three mountain ranges, and more than 50 miles of hiking trails? That's easy: South Mountain Park and Preserve.

Where: 10919 S. Central Ave., Phoenix, 602/495-5458, www.phoenix.gov/parks/trails/locations/south-mountain

Timing: The park's main entrance (free admission) opens daily at 5am and closes to new visitors at 7pm. Trail hours are 5am-11pm. The parking lot at Pima Canyon Trailhead (4800 E. Pima Canyon Rd., Phoenix) stays open until 9pm June 1-September 30. To drive to the highest point from the main entrance for sunset, give yourself 20 minutes before dusk; if you're hiking to the same spot, the trail is 5 miles (8 km) round-trip.

I could write an entire book solely about the best places in metro Phoenix to catch the sunset. I'm sure others have done it. My roundup might include the city's rooftop restaurants, definitely the Desert Botanical Garden, and maybe even my own front porch, which nestles up against the Phoenix Mountains Preserve. But nothing rivals the spectacular sunset as seen from **South Mountain Park and Preserve.**

Forming the southern lip of the valley bowl, the park's South Mountains comprise the ranges of Gila, Guadalupe, and Ma Ha Tauk. More than 16,000 acres of land ramble throughout these mountains. Trails for hiking, mountain biking, and horseback riding crawl up and over ridges, chisel through boulders, and stripe canyon floors, while motorists and cyclists wheel along the park's scenic roadways.

All that space and all that land add up to South Mountain Park and Preserve being one of the largest municipally managed parks in the nation.

It's also one of the most sacred. Within its expansive borders are thousands of petroglyphs etched into layers of stone by the Hohokam people. This prehistoric community dates from AD 200 to 1400, and though they didn't live within the South Mountains—in fact, they

▲ Bajada Hiking Trail

▲ South Mountain

▲ bicycling at sunset

resided in what is now Phoenix proper, establishing the large-scale irrigation canal system we still use today—they hunted, gathered, tended gardens, and performed ceremonies in the mountains.

The petroglyphs depict Hohokam life with representations of animals, birds, and people, plus geometric shapes that likely have symbolic meaning, though little is known (and much is argued) about the language and communication of the Hohokam people. You can see the rock art on several trails, including the Judith Tunnel Trail, Telegraph Pass Trail, Mormon Loop, Kiwanis Trail, and Holbert Trail.

The Holbert Trail not only leads you to the ancient messages of our region's earliest inhabitants, it also escorts you to the park's highest point: Dobbins Lookout, sitting pretty at 2,330 feet. It's here that you'll be treated to epic Arizona sunsets. Picture it: unobstructed views of the vast metro area awash in color, set against the craggy backdrop of the Sonoran Desert.

At Dobbins Lookout, tuck into the little stone hut—refurbished in 2020—that hugs the

▲ view of the Valley of the Sun from Dobbins Lookout

Silent Sunday

Every Sunday from 5am to 10am, South Mountain Park closes the main roadway at the 1-mile (1.6 km) point to all vehicle traffic. Great news for walkers, cyclers, joggers, dogs, meanderers, and anyone looking to stretch their legs on an uninterrupted ribbon of pavement through the park's desert vistas. Silent Sunday is offered year-round.

ledge or settle in on one of the benches that look out over the city. Watch the lights flicker on in the homes below and the planes at Sky Harbor lift off into the orange and pink clouds above.

You can hike the 2.5-mile (4 km) Holbert Trail to the peak, but remember, you'll have to hike back down the mountain after dark, so bring a headlamp. Another option is to drive Summit Road, a paved two-lane meander to the top from the main entrance on Central Avenue. This is usually how I do it—windows down, favorite tunes cued up, my gaze taking in every slice of the changing light.

Connect with...

7 Take a field trip on the Fresh Foodie Trail
14 Learn about Arizona's American Indian heritage at the Heard Museum
20 Lace up your boots for an urban hike on Trail 100

19 Play at the Musical Instrument Museum

Phoenix Essential • Art and Culture • Fun for Families and Kids

Why Go: Come see—er, hear—why the Musical Instrument Museum is one of the greatest music museums in the world, and the only one dedicated to the display of global musical instruments.

Where: 4725 E. Mayo Blvd., 480/478-6000, http://mim.org

Timing: The museum is open year-round, 9am-5pm daily. Plan for 3-4 hours to explore. Best times to visit: afternoons on weekdays and mornings on weekends; the galleries are busiest from 11am to 2pm.

It's very Phoenix to have James Beard Award-nominated restaurants in strip malls and international art collections at the airport. So even though the corner of the 101 Freeway and Mayo Boulevard seems like an unlikely home for a world-renowned museum, in Phoenix, that's just the way we do things.

The **Musical Instrument Museum** (MIM) isn't merely a roundup of old-timey violins and dusty pianos sitting in shadowy corners. Rated one of the top museums in the country, and an affiliate of the Smithsonian Institution, the MIM houses more than 13,600 instruments and related artifacts—of which nearly 7,000 are on display at any given time—from 200 countries and territories. Think an ancient paigu goblet drum from China's Neolithic period with a drumhead made of snakeskin, or a 10-string guitarra española, a Portuguese guitar from 1590.

And because music is meant to be heard, the MIM uses state-of-the-art technology not only to show instruments being played in their original context via video but also to deliver the sound right to guests' ears with wireless headsets. As you approach an exhibit, you'll hear the sounds of the instrument on display lilt, thrum, and twang in your headphones.

Former CEO of Target Corporation Robert Ulrich founded the two-story, 200,000-square-foot museum, which opened in 2010. His initial vision was to launch an art museum, but after his travels around the world, he discovered that most musical instrument

1: Musical Instrument Museum **2:** Musical Instrument Museum lobby **3:** a young listener **4:** live music

Sound *and* Sight

It's not only what you'll hear at MIM, it's what you'll see, too. The building's architecture thoughtfully reflects the spirit of the museum—raised shapes represent musical notes on the sandstone walls, windows look like piano keys, and the rotunda's curved lines mimic the elegant profile of a grand piano.

museums highlight Western instruments. So he hooked onto the idea of creating a museum dedicated to global, everyday instruments.

Curators collaborated with ethnomusicologists and other field experts to build the MIM's collection, traveling to remote locations to select instruments of fine construction, from reputed makers, with connections to influential performers, or because of special provenance.

Some of the instruments were still being actively played in their place of origin when they were donated by the musicians who owned them. Others were created by artisans exclusively for the MIM. Still others were purchased from previous collections.

There's a lot to see and do at the MIM, including year-round signature events and festivals. To get the most out of your visit, I suggest focusing on the following museum highlights.

Visit the **Geographic Galleries,** five galleries, each showcasing a world region—from Europe and Africa to Latin America, Asia and Oceania, and North America—display rare instruments (the world's largest playable sousaphone), artifacts (traditional clothing), and special exhibits (items from Fender and Steinway).

Head to the **Conservation Lab** where you can watch as experts carefully repair and maintain the museum's collection of instruments.

Don't miss the **Artist Gallery.** This gallery features rotating exhibits that showcase noteworthy instruments from famous musicians such as Maroon 5, Johnny Cash, and Elvis Presley.

The hands-on, interactive, family-friendly **Experience Gallery** lets you play a theremin, strum a harp, bang a gong, and more. Also stop by the **Encore Gallery,** which is similar

Experience Gallery at the Musical Instrument Museum

to the Experience Gallery, but features developmentally appropriate instruments and activities for little ones (ages 4-8).

Finally, the **MIM Music Theater** hosts a year-round calendar of live musical performances in the 300-seat theater.

Connect with...

4 Tour Taliesin West

14 Learn about Arizona's American Indian heritage at the Heard Museum

21 Dive into the blues and R&B music scene

20 Lace up your boots for an urban hike on Trail 100

Outdoor Adventures • Fun for Families and Kids

Why Go: Trail 100 merges city life and desert wilderness on an 11-mile (18 km) hike that ascends the peaks of the Phoenix Mountains Preserve, tunnels under streets and highways, and wends past striking views of the downtown skyline.

Where: Point-to-point trail through the Phoenix Mountains Preserve • Can be hiked in either direction, starting from the trailhead at Tatum Boulevard south of Double-tree Ranch Road or from Mountain View Park (9901 N. 7th Ave., Phoenix) • www.phoenix.gov/parks/trails

Timing: To hike the entirety of the trail, allot for 4-5 hours, depending on your ability. Because Trail 100 passes through the heart of the city, there are numerous trailheads along the way that allow you to hop on and off. To enjoy sunrise, start from Mountain View Park and hike east. For sunset, begin from the trailhead at Tatum Boulevard.

It may not seem like it, what with our highways and shopping centers and high-rises, but Phoenix boasts 41,000 acres of mountain preserves and desert parks. This is no small feat for a metro area of nearly 5 million people. Our valley location means that from north to south and east to west, mountains ring our borders, natural areas that can be hiked and biked on more than 200 miles (320 km) of trails.

Thanks to its iconic shape, Camelback Mountain gets all the attention, especially from tourists. On any given day, throngs of out-of-towners inch their way to the summit from dawn to dusk. It's a bucket-list hike for many—and one I encourage everyone to do at least once—but if you're seeking a hike that serves up good challenges, epic views, and few crowds, it's **Trail 100** all the way.

Officially named the Charles M. Christiansen Memorial Trail, the 11-mile route is the longest trek in the Phoenix Mountains Preserve. It's located smack in the middle of the city, and this area of the preserve claims notable landmarks like Shaw Butte, North Mountain, and its highest peak, Piestewa.

Trail 100 offers beautiful vistas.

The land was originally mined for mercury and used for cattle grazing until the late 1950s when it was annexed for preservation. Much of the metamorphic rock—a granite known as schist—throughout the mountains dates back more than 14 million years.

Take note of the rock's shifting hues and morphing shapes as you hike. Along portions of the trail west of Cave Creek Road, the landscape looks like an ancient lava field, ebony chunks of sediment layering the earth. In other areas the rock gleams white and smooth. There's even a section between Shea Boulevard and Dreamy Draw Recreation Area that resembles a gigantic dried coral reef; here, it's easy to imagine Phoenix as a once watery city deep in the ocean.

I've hiked end to end several times, and I always start at Mountain View Park and traverse the route east. The trail is mostly flat starting out, but as soon as you enter the tunnel under 7th Street and emerge into a mesquite-shaded arbor, you start to ascend into the hills. A plateau affords unmarred sightlines of the city skyline.

Continuing east, another tunnel shuttles you under Cave Creek Road to a picturesque

Piestewa Peak on Trail 100

desert in the North 32nd neighborhood. Keep your eyes open for a roaming coyote or two. I've also seen rattlesnakes sunning themselves on the trail in spring.

The trail gets steeper and rockier as you near Dreamy Draw Recreation Area, but the views get better too. You'll tunnel under AZ 51 into a "forest" of creosote bushes, mesquite trees, and, come spring, wildflowers.

As you climb up and out of Dreamy Draw, the trail travels through the most remote parts of the preserve. At the 40th Street Trailhead, more hikers will join you; there's a popular summit with a bird's-eye view of Paradise Valley. Keep journeying east to Tatum Boulevard, where you'll exit at a small parking lot.

Some of the best parts about this hike are the visitor centers and recreation areas along the way; in other words, ideal places for water and bathroom breaks. Check out **North Mountain Visitor Center** (12950 N. 7th St., Phoenix), **Dreamy Draw Recreation Area** (2421 E. Northern Ave., Phoenix), and **40th Street Trailhead** (9200 N. 40th St., Phoenix).

Connect with...

26 Bike the Loop

31 Summit "A" Mountain at sunrise

41 Enjoy desert blooms and autumn leaves

21 Dive into the blues and R&B scene

Local Scenes • Art and Culture

Why Go: Like most things worth seeking, Phoenix's live blues and R&B scene flies under the radar and is stacked with talent. You just have to know where to go.

Where: Visit these clubs throughout Phoenix.

Timing: You can find weekly live blues and R&B shows at Phoenix-area clubs, bars, and lounges all year long. Shows feature local musicians as well as national acts. Friday and Saturday nights are your best bet to catch the music, with doors typically opening at 8pm. Most venues set a cash-only cover charge of $7-15.

Every Sunday night, my husband and I turn on the radio. Yes—the radio. We power down our laptops and our streaming services and our smartphones (OK, not those), and we set the dial to local radio show ***Those Lowdown Blues.***

Hosted on Phoenix's 91.5 KJZZ (https://kjzz.org/blues-playlist) since 1984, the show takes listeners on a five-hour journey into the record collection of renowned blues harmonica player Bob Corritore. Corritore pulls albums from the hundreds that line his living room walls from floor to ceiling to cull a unique playlist that he shares on the air. His shows usually revolve around a loose theme, and between songs Corritore shares his deep knowledge about the genre, as well as real-life anecdotes from his decades-long music career.

The blues musician moved to Phoenix in 1981 from Chicago, and, like all Phoenix transplants, Corritore brought with him the tastes and culture of his hometown. This included Corritore's signature Chicago blues-style harp playing.

It is musicians like Corritore—players coming from Chicago, Memphis, Mississippi—who have created Phoenix's sound: a bit-of-everything blend. At Corritore's roots and blues concert club, **The Rhythm Room** (1019 E. Indian School Rd., Phoenix, 602/265-4842, https://rhythmroom.com), which he opened in 1991 to host national and local acts, you'll hear horn-heavy Memphis soul, some boogie-woogie piano or Delta blues harmonica,

△ Beyonce and Jay-Z mural by Giovannie "Just" Dixon

△ throwback cocktails at The Womack

△ The bands enter here at the Rhythm Room.

a touch of Motown kicked off with up-tempo jump and jive, and maybe even a country twang or two.

The Phoenix sound has been decades in the making. The city has had a thriving blues scene since the 1930s, when dance clubs on the south side hosted jazz musicians and, later in the 1940s, blues artists. Traveling musicians on their way to California used Phoenix as a waystation to perform and record music, swirling styles and sharing different techniques.

Arizona's blues veteran Lewis Paul "Big Pete" Pearson arrived from Austin in the 1950s and has been fronting Phoenix bands with his soulful croon ever since. Today he's considered Phoenix's King of the Blues, having shared the stage with legends like Ray Charles, Etta James, and Muddy Waters, and rubbing elbows with Elvis Presley (at a performance near Fort Hood) and Michael Jackson (when Pearson lived next door to Jackson's grandmother). And Pearson and Bob Corritore have been playing together since they met 40 years ago.

In addition to The Rhythm Room, you can visit several other local nightspots that showcase blues, R&B, soul, funk, and Motown. Stop by **American Legion Post 65 Canteen**

Rhythm Room

For Your Collection

The compilation album *Flying' High: A Collection of Phoenix Blues, Rhythm, and Spirit* from 2010 is essential listening for Phoenix music fans. It features 27 tunes—12 of them previously unreleased—all recorded by artists in Phoenix in the 1950s and '60s. You'll hear everything from high-energy gospel and lowdown blues to soul and doo-wop.

(1624 E. Broadway Rd., Phoenix, 602/628-6059, https://twilliamspost65.org), a no-frills joint with live music every Sunday night and cards and dominoes on Wednesdays.

Head to **The Womack** (5749 N. 7th St., Phoenix, 602/283-5232, www.thewomack.us), a throwback cocktail lounge with drinks like gin rickeys and sidecars. Saturday nights feature local act The Roscoe Taylor Band with Jimmie McElroy, whose R&B, funk, and soul tunes get everyone on the dance floor.

Visit **Solo's Café** (5025 N. 7th Ave., Phoenix, 602/265-1955, www.facebook.com/solo-scafe1) for strong spirits and excellent Friday night catfish along with the R&B, Motown, and funk stylings of the great Laydee Jai.

The sophisticated **Boom Boom Room** (1544 E. McDowell Rd., Phoenix, www.face-book.com/boomboomroomphx) spins old-school hip-hop and current R&B in an intimate setting. Can't find it? Look for the mural of Beyoncé and Jay-Z that graces the building.

Connect with...

9 Buy authentic American Indian art
11 Feast on soul food at Mrs. White's Golden Rule Café
19 Play at the Musical Instrument Museum

22 Shop local

Shopping • Local Scenes

Why Go: There's no better place than a locally owned shop to discover the one-of-a-kind treasures from some of Arizona's best makers, artists, designers, and artisans.

Where: Visit these local shops around Phoenix.

Timing: The main four stores are open year-round, seven days a week, with the exception of Straw & Wool, which offers regular hours Wed.-Sun., but is open by appointment Monday and Tuesday. Even though these stores are small in size, they stock a lot of diverse items. Plan to spend an hour or two shopping at each place.

When you think of U.S. cities with a distinct sense of style, places like New York (sophisticated), Portland (quirky-cool), and Miami (bold and colorful) come to mind. Those are destinations with a "look" you can identify, one that expresses something specific about the city, its people, and its character.

Phoenix, on the other hand, is less easy to pin down. It serves up a shape-shifting personality influenced by our constantly changing population. People move in; people move out. With that comes a tidal ebb and flow of new perspectives and fresh ideas.

There are some recurring themes, though. Desert influences abound (saguaro-adorned ceramics, sunset-hued tees, stark desert watercolors), as do sunny-day fashions in breezy fabrics and light colors. Mexican sugar skulls show up on skirts, and formalwear leans more resort casual than black tie.

Some might argue that this melting pot of inspiration indicates an absence of style. I'd argue the opposite. We're a town defined by rebirth, which allows for young entrepreneurs, artists, makers, and first-time business owners to carve their own path.

Just browse any of the city's independent stores, most of them women-owned, BIPOC-owned, and LGBTQ+-owned, to see the artistic expression of our city. The following are my suggestions for not-to-miss shops.

Rachel Malloy, founder of Bunky Boutique

Phoenix General

▲ Phoenix General

Rachel Malloy opened **Bunky Boutique** (1001 N. Central Ave., Ste. 125, Phoenix, https://bunkyboutique.com) in a teeny space on Roosevelt Row in 2007. Since then, the shop has moved locations twice and expanded to Phoenix Sky Harbor Airport. But even with the moves and growth, Malloy has remained committed to showcasing products made by locals. The best example of this is the store's AZ Love line featuring men's and women's T-shirts (I own two), totes (bought several), hats (my husband has a gray one), and children's gear—all sporting the state's outline with a heart marking Phoenix.

Hauz of Smalls (1817 E. Indian School Rd., Phoenix, https://hauzofsmalls.com) believes that "good taste can't be defined by size nor gender," and the shop echoes that tagline's sentiment in its all-inclusive offerings of drag merch, unisex fashions, fun home decor, and jewelry and art by LGBTQ+ artists.

From jewelry by Arizona's Heliotrope to handmade leather wallets and bags from Phoenix's Ezra Arthur, **Phoenix General** (5538 N. 7th St., #120, Phoenix, 602/237-6922, and 214 E. Roosevelt St., Phoenix, 623/248-8686; https://phxgeneral.com) is a veritable who's who of local makers. This was always the mission of Kenny Barrett, who owns the store with his partner Joshua Hahn. Part art gallery, part cooperative retail space, Phoenix Gen (as it's known by regulars) also supports local causes. For example, when they sold their "Generic Queer" T-shirts, a reproduction of a 1980s-era Pride March shirt, they donated the proceeds to the human rights campaign.

For Ali Nervis, first came Archwood Exchange, a nonprofit that hosts the monthly Buy Black Marketplace. Then came **Straw & Wool** (610 E. Roosevelt St., Unit 144, Phoenix, https://strawandwool.com). The latter is the hip downtown haberdashery that Nervis co-owns with Henry Dickerson and Dominic Clark. The trio started Archwood as a swap meet to feature Black-owned businesses, but they soon found a niche in hats. Straw & Wool works with more than a dozen designers to stock unique toppers in styles ranging from boaters and Panamas to the popular red-bottomed hats.

Other local faves include **Frances** (10 W. Camelback Rd., Phoenix, 602/279-5467, www.shopfrancesboutique.com) for stationery, **Local Nomad** (100 E. Camelback Rd., #168, Phoenix, 602/441-4378, www.localnomadshop.com) for candles and gifts, **Practical Art** (5070 N. Central Ave., Phoenix, 602/264-1414, https://practical-art.com) for edgy works of art, and **Made Art Boutique** (922 N. 5th St., Phoenix, 602/256-6233, www.madephx.com) for everything artisan-crafted.

Connect with...

⑤ Discover new writers at local bookstores
⑪ Feast on soul food at Mrs. White's Golden Rule Cafe

23 **Soak up city views at Wrigley Mansion**

Fun for Families and Kids • Art and Culture

Why Go: The iconic Spanish Colonial estate built by chewing gum mogul William Wrigley Jr. crowns a hilltop in the center of Phoenix, commanding unrivaled views in every direction.

Where: 2501 E. Telewa Trail, Phoenix, 602/955-4079, https://wrigleymansion.com

Timing: Guided tours ($17/person, reservations required) of the mansion are hosted Wednesday-Sunday at 2pm. Tours last 45-60 minutes. You can also experience the property at the on-site restaurants. Geordie's offers brunch, lunch, and dinner, plus wine, beer, and cocktails in the lounge. Christopher's serves dinner.

Trivia question: What do chewing gum and SPAM have in common? Answer: The Wrigley Mansion.

You wouldn't know it to look at the Phoenix manor, what with its hand-painted domed ceiling, curved staircase, Catalina tiles, 12 bathrooms—some with plush seating nooks—and 24 rooms, each more grand than the last. (Did I mention the fireplaces? Total count tops out at 11.)

But yes, it's true. The Wrigley Mansion was home to both chewing gum and SPAM royalty. In 1932, William Wrigley Jr., of Wrigley Chewing Gum, built the estate as a gift to his wife Ada. In 1992, George "Geordie" Hormel, heir of Hormel Foods, bought it to save it from being razed by the city.

At 16,000 square feet, the home sprawls and spreads in delicious luxury. Ornate hallways lead to interior balconies that overlook living spaces. Art deco chandeliers drip from ceilings. Foil—the very same that wrapped Wrigley's gum—papers the wall. A secret stairway ducks under a private patio.

And everywhere in the house live artifacts and treasures from the Wrigley and Hormel families. You can read the original letters, now framed and hanging in the entrance, written from William Wrigley to the builders during the construction phase, which started in 1929.

the grand entrance of Wrigley Mansion

▲ Christopher's Restaurant at Wrigley Mansion

Geordie Hormel's art collection crowds the upper rooms' walls. His family photos line the hallway. You can even play a few tunes on the Wrigley's 1920s-era Steinway piano, one of only two privately owned Steinways in existence.

You could spend hours poring over the immaculately cared-for contents inside the home, but the real gift of the Wrigley Mansion is the view.

Capping a 100-foot-high hill in the middle of Phoenix, the house's rippled-glass windows, wraparound porches, and second-story balconies gaze out at some of the most notable landmarks in the city: Camelback Mountain, the Arizona Biltmore (also owned by Wrigley), Papago Buttes, and the downtown skyline.

Over the years, I've enjoyed this panorama many ways. Once, during an early morning jog along the Arizona Canal, my husband and I darted off the dirt path to run up the mansion's winding driveway. The steep climb rewarded us with the sight of the city bathed in the sun's rising glow. Another time, we invited my mother for happy hour at Geordie's. When our server suggested we take our glasses of wine and wander the mansion, we jumped at the

Join the Club

A little-known quirk about Wrigley Mansion: Due to its locale smack dab in the middle of residential homes, the city of Phoenix requires that it operate as a private club. Even though you don't need a membership to visit, Wrigley Mansion sells them anyway in order to officially remain open to the public. A mere 20 bucks a year gets you mansion access, invites to VIP events, priority restaurant reservations, and free valet parking.

chance, eventually making our way to one of the east-facing balconies. Though I've not yet done it, you can also join a guided tour, which pairs all those outstanding views with historical and architectural tidbits.

William Wrigley died shortly after the mansion was built, but the Wrigley family owned the property for decades, inviting esteemed guests like U.S. presidents, dignitaries, and celebrities. When Geordie Hormel and his wife Jamie purchased the house in the 1990s, they opened it up for the rest of us to enjoy.

Connect with...

4 Tour Taliesin West

15 Explore Phoenix's mid-century modern architecture

18 Watch the sun set at South Mountain Park

24 Taste Tucson's global flavors

Tucson Essential • Drink and Dine

Why Go: Tucson may be a mid-sized American city, but you'd never know it by its international culinary offerings. Adventurous eaters can nosh their way around the world—from Eritrea and Bosnia to Jamaica and El Salvador—all within Tucson city limits.

Where: Stop by one of my favorite spots for delicious food.

Timing: Lunch is the best meal to eat at these places—you can join the crowd of regulars, which is a nice way to get a sense of each restaurant's personality and clientele. All of these places are small and popular, so be prepared to wait for a table. But once you're seated, service is usually quick.

It seems like every city claims to be a foodie destination. But not many places can say they're a UNESCO City of Gastronomy.

UNESCO introduced the category of Gastronomy for its Creative Cities Network in 2005 with the inaugural title going to Popayan, Colombia. There are only 116 destinations that are part of the Creative Cities Network, and of those, only 6 are in the United States. And Tucson is the only one that's a City of Gastronomy.

Tucson earned the coveted honor by being more than a roundup of great restaurants (although that doesn't hurt) and a bunch of culinary awards (again, not a bad thing). No, Tucson earned its title because the city deeply supports its food cultures—traditional and nontraditional, local and international—and takes care to make sure that dining in Tucson reflects a meaningful sense of place.

That sense of place includes the far-flung origins of people who've traveled the world to find refuge in Tucson, making a new home here.

People like Amanuel Gebremariam, who opened a restaurant to serve his ancestral cuisine. **Zemam's** (2731 E. Broadway Blvd., 520/323-9928, and 119 E. Speedway Blvd., 520/882-4955, www.zemamsrestaurants.com, $18) has been offering Ethiopian food to Tucsonans for

spicy jerk chicken

okra

fried plantains

Salvadoran pupusa

more than 25 years. Gebremariam makes the restaurant's *injera*—a fermented bread central to Ethiopian cuisine—from a grain called *teff*, and he uses his mother's recipes for many of the dishes, like the *doro wat* (chicken stew) seasoned with lemon and steeped in spices.

Another chef dipping into his mother's cookbook is Jamaican-born Duwayne Hall. He's the owner and chef of **D's Island Grill** (3156 E. Fort Lowell Rd., 520/861-2271, www.dsislandgrill.com, $16), a tiny restaurant with boisterous energy and gospel music pumping through the speakers. Hall not only uses his mom's recipes, but he also learned to cook from her. Menu highlights include charcoal-grilled jerk chicken with an in-house blended sauce, braised oxtail, and bread sweetened with cinnamon.

The owner of **Alafia West African Cuisine** (1070 N. Swan Rd., 520/331-7161, $10), Ismael Lawani, hails from the West African country of Benin. When you visit his restaurant, he'll greet you in English and French—the official language of his home country. Lawani uses all West African recipes, like the 20-spiced goat soup and the barbecued tilapia with fried plantains. Interestingly, ingredients like okra make frequent appearances in dishes, and

▲ injera bread

Saving Seeds

Because of the biodiversity of the region's desert borderlands, there are more heritage foods grown within 100 miles of Tucson than any other city in North America. Shop **Native Seeds/SEARCH** (520/622-0830, www.nativeseeds.org) to grow these foods in your own garden. The nonprofit seed bank conserves heirloom seeds found throughout the Southwest, then sells them ($3.25/packet).

though long associated with U.S. Southern cuisine, use of them in cooking is an African tradition.

From El Salvador, there's Luis Gonzalez, owner of **Selena's Salvadorian Restaurant** (2513 N. Campbell Ave., 520/278-4090, $15). Chef and business partner Sandra Gonzalez brings her El Salvador roots to life with authentic eats like *caldo de res* (beef broth with cabbage, potatoes, carrots, squash, and corn), *pastelitos* (crispy empanadas stuffed with ground beef), and of course, *pupusas*. If you've never had a pupusa, picture a corn flatbread filled with all sorts of goodies. Gonzalez offers several varieties, crowning them with fermented slaw and spicy salsa.

Tucson's multicultural present owes much to its multicultural past, a vibrant tapestry of Indigenous and Mexican food heritages. And, of course, those cuisines are here, too. Along with Thai and Argentinian and Puerto Rican and Sri Lankan, and a whole lot more.

Connect with...

28 Hunt for murals
32 Savor Sonoran-style food
34 Stroll the Heirloom Farmers Market at Rillito Park

25 Honor the dead at the All Souls Procession

Tucson Essential • Local Scenes

Why Go: The All Souls Procession is a 30-years-strong tradition of remembrance that converges every year in the heart of the Old Pueblo.

Where: Events take place at and around Mercado San Agustin • 100 S. Avenida del Convento, Tucson, 520/461-1107, https://mercadodistrict.com • https://allsoulsprocession.org

Timing: The multiday celebration takes place the first weekend in November. Friday night kicks off with Night of the Living Fest (from $20 per person) at 4pm. Saturday's Procession of the Little Angels (free) runs 3pm-7pm. The All Souls Procession Grand Finale (free) is Sunday 4pm-10pm. The parade route follows the Santa Cruz River, starting on Grande Avenue south of Speedway Boulevard and concluding at Mercado San Agustin.

Though the literal translation of Dia de Los Muertos is "Day of the Dead"—a morbid-sounding description if ever there was one—the actual event is anything but.

The Mexican holiday (associated with the Catholic celebration of All Saints' Day on November 1) is a time when friends and family come together to pay tribute to those loved ones who have passed on. It's a way to commemorate both life *and* death, and as anyone who's participated in the holiday can attest, it's a powerful revelry of remembrance.

Tucson honors its Mexican roots with the **All Souls Procession,** a three-day festival inspired by Dia de Los Muertos. The nonprofit arts collective Many Mouths One Stomach (MMOS) coordinates the volunteer-led event, which has generated nearly $30 million for the Tucson arts community over the past 30 years.

As dusk falls on the city, you'll see children clutching photos of deceased pets. You'll see sons and daughters holding treasured mementos of parents who've died. Veterans honor fallen troop members; astronomers mourn the loss of Pluto's planet status; groups remember endangered animals. People experience the event dressed in regular clothes or outfitted in full costume and face paint. They hold tokens of loved ones and tuck urns into backpacks.

a huge urn filled with photos of the dead, notes, and prayers

All Souls Procession

Attendees join the Procession in full makeup.

No matter their reason for attending the procession or for whom they miss, everybody and every soul walk side by side in grief—and in celebration of life.

Sunday's finale procession showcases elaborately designed floats, *papier mâché* puppets, art installations, photo collages, live performances, stilt walkers, seven-foot-tall sugar skulls, portable altars, and decorated shrines.

To participate, all you have to do is show up. You can choose to join the procession, a 1.5-mile (2.4 km) walk led by a huge urn filled with names and photos of the dead, affectionate notes and messages to them, and well-wishes and prayers. Or you can simply witness the collective contemplation. The procession concludes with a ceremonial lighting of the urn. As the contents are set ablaze, a crane lifts the urn 30 feet high for the mourners to see.

This grassroots gathering is many things. It's a public funeral. It's an art exhibition. It's a sacred parade. And most importantly, it's a festival of compassion that unites a city and creates a community.

The first procession took place in 1990 when a local artist honored her father's recent

honoring the dead at the All Souls Procession

Breaking Bread

The Mexican *panaderías* in Tucson take part in the All Souls Procession, too. Stop by for freshly baked *pan de muertos*. These are "sweet breads of the dead," delicious—and beautiful—skull-shaped and skeleton-shaped cakes and pastries. I like **La Estrella Bakery** (5266 S. 12th Ave., 520/741-0656, www.laestrellabakeryincaz.com).

death with performance art and a community altar. Her public mourning drew a crowd of about 30 people. Today, the All Souls Procession attracts hundreds of thousands of participants from all walks of life, making it one of the largest celebrations of its kind in the country. The event's inclusivity and diversity—people of all religions, traditions, creed, and color join the celebration—speaks volumes about the universal experience of death.

Connect with...

28 Hunt for murals
29 Join La Fiesta de Los Vaqueros
33 See mermaids on Fourth Avenue

26 Bike the Loop

Why Go: You're not a real Tucsonan if you haven't biked The Loop. Period.

Where: Access points for The Loop are located throughout metro Tucson • 520/724-5000, https://webcms.pima.gov/government/the_loop

Timing: If you have 5-8 hours, you could bike the entirety of The Loop, but for casual cyclists, I recommend picking a section for a 60-90-minute ride. The best time of day is morning and evening, especially in summer, but during the winter, you can enjoy The Loop all day. Dress in layers, wear sunscreen, and bring water.

My preferred form of exercise is running. I'm an avid runner, hitting the trails, roads, and greenbelts as often as I can. I say this not to brag, but merely to clarify that cycling, for me, is purely recreational. I own a road bike, but I rarely drag it down from the hooks in the garage. Instead, I hop on my pink-and-white cruiser, complete with a basket and trilling bell. Then I just . . . well, cruise.

And when you want to cruise, there's no better place than **The Loop** in Tucson. Officially named the Chuck Huckelberry Loop, the nearly 140-mile (225 km) system of paved, shared-use pathways links metro Tucson with Marana and Oro Valley. It also connects the Santa Cruz, Pantano, and Rillito River Parks with the Julian Wash and Harrison Road Greenways.

It's considered to be relatively new, having been fully completed in 2018, but its origins date to 1983. In the aftermath of particularly bad floods that year, Pima County reinforced the dirt walls of the Rillito, Pantano, and Santa Cruz riverbeds with soil-cement embankments and created access roads to help with regular maintenance. Local residents began using the unpaved roads for dog walking, jogging, biking, and morning strolls. Realizing the added community benefit of the flood-control project, the county started building parks along the rivers with pathways to reach them. By 1986, a paved section on the Rillito River leading to Rillito River Park was completed. The Loop was born.

biking near downtown Tucson

Today there are dozens of access points throughout the city, so no matter where you are, you'll likely find an easy spot to hop on The Loop. (Visit the website for a map; the site offers links to a PDF version as well as an interactive one.)

Whether you're experiencing The Loop on two feet or two wheels (as long as it doesn't have a motor, any mode of transport is good to go, even horses), you're guaranteed to see desert flora and fauna—from wildflowers to ocotillos, from jackrabbits to hummingbirds—as well as urban sights such as restaurants, shops, and farmers markets.

The best part of The Loop? All the public art that graces the route, nearly 50 pieces in total. Look for an arrow painted on the pavement pointing to the art, or download a gallery map from the website. A few notable artworks: a sculpture by Chris Tanz titled *Joining Hands* that arches over the Julian Wash as a symbol of unity; Vicki Scuri's *Agave Walls*, a bright green wall in shapes inspired by the succulent, which lines the Rillito River Bridge and pops against the desert's muted tones; *Batty Biker Family*, a steel sculpture on the south

Rattlesnake Bridge in Tucson

Love the Loop

The volunteer-run **Pima County Parklands Foundation** (520/241-8885, http:// pimaparklands.org) works hard to help protect and enhance the parks and green spaces in Pima County, including The Loop. Where public funding fails, Parklands steps in. Consider making a tax-deductible donation to lend a helping hand.

bank of the Rillito River by artist Stephen Fairfield, designed to pay homage to the bridge where the local bats roost.

In its tethering together of parks and trails, bus and bike routes, offices and schools, hotels and concert venues, The Loop creates a vibrant work-life-play community all along the way.

Connect with...

28 Hunt for murals

30 Raise your glass at historic bars

34 Stroll the Heirloom Farmers Market at Rillito Park

27 Outfit yourself in custom Western boots

Tucson Essential • Shopping

Why Go: As one of the few remaining makers of fully handmade boots in the United States (outside Texas and Tennessee, anyway), Stewart Boot Company crafts boots to last a lifetime.

Where: Stewart Boot Company • 30 W. 28th St., Tucson, 520/622-2706

Timing: Stewart Boot Company is open Mon.-Thurs. Reservations are recommended. If you're shopping on a whim, no worries, but do call ahead. Once you're fitted and your order is taken, expect about six months before you receive the finished product.

I purchased my first pair of cowgirl boots on discount at a store-closing blowout sale, half a size too big, and in a hipster college town far from ranches and rodeo grounds. If it's true that a classic Western boot says a lot about the wearer, then these clearly announced: "I have no money, and I'm trying too hard."

But a custom pair of boots. Now that's the way to go.

There are many reasons why. Some are obvious—durability, longevity, an ideal fit suited to your exact foot size and shape—and some are less so. Such as: beautifully designed, customized boots, like a perfect tattoo, can be a powerful expression of who you are.

When you meet with a boot artisan—a maker in a Western tradition hundreds of years old—you'll understand why. They can elevate boots from basic footwear into an art form that captures your very essence. Silver or flower inlays. Supple or tough leather. Decorative tops in colorful designs or serious styles in subdued hues. Braided piping. Signature stitching. Detailed tooling. Box toes or wing tips, in-the-mud work boots or dance-hall-ready fancy boots.

In Tucson, you'll want to visit **Stewart Boot Company,** a company known for hand-making every boot, during every step of the process. Situated in a nondescript industrial complex, the shop was opened in 1940 by master boot maker Ronnie Stewart. In 1970,

Western boots

Boots can do double duty as fashion statement and work footwear.

Victor Borg assumed ownership and continued the thriving company, at one point operating with 44 makers crafting 1,000 pairs of boots a month for 150 stores in 35 states.

Today, business is steady but smaller. Victor and his wife Linda do the sizing, stretching, and stitching; a handful of other boot makers round out the crew. Nothing is outsourced, and nothing is factory made. The leather is tanned locally, and dyed all the way through—a trick to ensure boots maintain their color—and it's pre-shrunk in pieces so rain will never alter the final fit of the boot (not so much a problem for us Arizonans).

If you're new to the boot scene, don't worry. The staff at Stewart will guide you. They'll ask questions about what type of leather you're looking for (cowhide or alligator), heel height, toe shape (square or tapered), color (black, maybe pink?), and most importantly, design (an eagle etched in the leather, perhaps). Then they'll measure your foot and take your order.

Borg makes boots for rodeo cowboys and cowgirls, area ranchers, and local Tucsonans, and has loyal customers who return year after year to grow their boot collection. Borg has

These Boots Are Made for Road-Trippin'

When you desire custom boots and you're in the mood for a drive, head to Nogales, Arizona. **Paul Bond Boots** (915 W. Paul Bond Dr., 520/281-0512, www.paulbondboots. com) has been making custom kicks in high-quality leathers since 1946. Notable people who've donned Paul Bond Boots include Reba McEntire, Linda Ronstadt, Paul Newman, and Kevin Costner.

also designed boots for famous folks like Arnold Schwarzenegger and Clint Eastwood. But no matter your celebrity status, a handcrafted boot requires time and patience—a pair of Stewart Boots can take anywhere from three to six months to complete.

Custom boots aren't cheap either, with prices starting around $450. But unlike other shoes that thin and wear over time, Western boots fit better with every scuff of the heel and softening of the leather.

Connect with...

㉙ Join La Fiesta de Los Vaqueros

㉚ Raise your glass at historic bars

㉟ Transform your backyard with desert plants

28 Hunt for murals

Art and Culture • Native Cultures

Why Go: A mural tour of downtown Tucson never gets old, as artists continually refresh public spaces with powerful artworks of astounding size and beauty. Some pieces depict the Sonoran Desert, some beloved famous figures, and others cultural traditions.

Where: Stroll through Tucson to find can't-miss murals.

Timing: There are hundreds of murals throughout downtown Tucson, and dozens more around the metro area; you could spend two days tracking them all down. This guide includes seven downtown murals totaling a 2-mile (3 km) walk, plus an additional mural within driving distance south of downtown. Plan to visit during daylight when you can appreciate the vibrant colors and designs of each artist's work.

Tucson has some famous murals, such as the oft-photographed *Tranquil Lady* (246 N. 4th Ave.) by **Ignacio Garcia** (http://artebyignacio.com) or the rotating murals at Rialto Theatre (318 E. Congress St.), a must for Instagrammers. The city's muralists come from diverse backgrounds, like Tohono O'odham tribal member **Quinton Antone;** from wide-ranging professions, such as tattoo artist **Clint Tzu** (@clint_tzu) or photographer **Andy Burgess** (www.andyburgessart.com, @andyartist100); and with various messages to share, like those of LGBTQ+ activist **Valyntina Grenier** (www.valyntinagrenier.com, @valyntinagrenier).

Jessica Gonzales (www.jessicagonzalesart.com, @jessicagonzalesart) is one of my favorite Tucson muralists. I can't get enough of her dreamy *Beauty of the Monsoon Season* (17th Street and 9th Street) or the happy-faced woman bearing a crown of flowers (720 W. Silverlake Rd.). There's something inherently joyful about Gonzales's work that I love.

The best way to find *your* favorite muralist? Take a self-guided tour. I've cobbled together an easy stroll of a few must-see murals.

Stop 1: *Greetings From Tucson* (406 N. 6th Ave)

Victor Ving and **Lisa Beggs** (www.greetingstour.com) have been traveling the coun-

 *Travel for All* by Ash White at the Hotel McCoy

▲ colorful Black Lives Matter mural by Camila Ibarra

▲ mural by Randy L. Barton in the Mercado District

try since 2015 to create large-scale "greetings" art. On this piece on the back wall of Miller's Surplus, Tucson tagger turned muralist **Rock Martinez** (www.cyfiart.com, @cyfione) added his own touches inside the letter C.

Stop 2: *Why I Love Where I Live* (234 E. 6th St.)

Kristin Tovar, co-founder of the popular local store Why I Love Where I Live, commissioned these two murals, both painted on Tucson's 106th birthday. Artist **Danny Martin** painted one in homage to Tovar, who fell in love with the city while taking photos of it. The other mural, also by Martin, is a tribute to Los Apson, a 1960s-era Mexican rock band from Sonora.

Stop 3: *Sonora* (300 E. University Blvd.)

Costa Rican artist **Karlito Miller Espinosa,** aka **Mata Ruda** (@mataruda), teaches illustration at the University of Arizona, and he designed this piece with his students Analaura Villegas and Brisa Tzintzun. A woman's face is the main focus, but the patchwork designs behind her represent the organizations that use the building.

Stop 4: *Jack and Bill* (318 E. Congress)

On the upper east wall of the Rialto Theatre, **Ignacio Garcia** painted Hall of Fame basketball player Bill Walton riding the mythical jackalope (a jackrabbit with antelope horns). The 75-foot-high mural is one of eight completed as part of the Tucson Mural Arts Program.

Stop 5: *Vergiss* (178 E. Broadway Blvd.)

Irish artist **Fin DAC** (https://findac.tumblr.com) is known for painting women from East Asian cultures with an intent to subvert long-held stereotypes. This beautiful piece—all bold oranges and teals—covers the brick wall of The Lewis Hotel.

Stop 6: *Running of the Piñatas* (31 N. 6th Ave.)

Another mural by **Ignacio Garcia,** this one on the south side of the UPS store, depicts a boy running from a pack of piñatas. One of four commissioned by the Tucson Arts Brigade

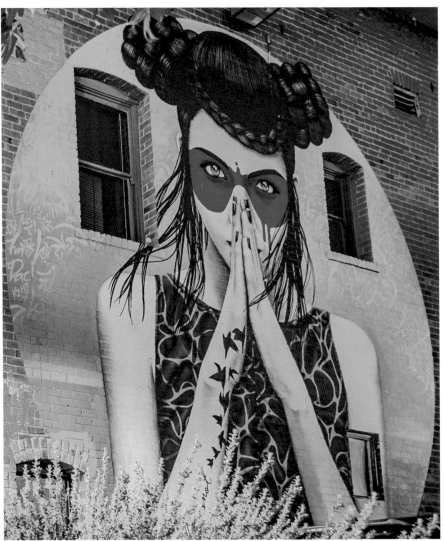

Vergiss by Fin DAC

Downtown Mural project, the mural captures Garcia's childhood memory of once being chased by a bull on his grandfather's ranch.

Stop 7: *Goddess of the Agave* (440 N. 7th Ave.)

On the west wall of the Benjamin Plumbing Supply building, **Rock Martinez** painted a 50- by 54-foot likeness of his girlfriend. Blue-green cactuses bloom orange flowers at the bottom of the mural, and an agave plant sprouts at the top. The mural is so iconic that its image now shows up in everything from the bus schedule to tourism videos.

Stop 8: *Selena* (1439 S. 4th Ave.)

While this mural of Tejano singer Selena Quintanilla-Pérez isn't within walking distance of the others, I included it because it's just perfect. Artist **Jonny Ballesteros** (@jonnybubonik) created the gold-framed mural as a tribute to the gone-but-not-forgotten Selena, and it was envisioned with help by **Lower Arizona** (@lower_arizona), an Instagram account that celebrates Mexican hip-hop culture.

Goddess of the Agave by Rock Martinez

Art for All

When it comes to celebrated art forms, murals are perhaps the most egalitarian of them all. Liberated from the confines of an elite gallery, inexpensive to create, and absent a costly price tag. In other words: Murals are free to enjoy and available to everyone. In a city known for lifting up disparate voices, whether through art or food or culture, it's not surprising that Tucson offers its buildings and streets as a citywide canvas for creatives to express themselves. Take the **Hotel McCoy** (720 W. Silverlake Rd., Tucson, 844/782-9622, www.hotelmccoy.com, $90/night), for example. Its lobby showcases art, where every piece is for sale (and affordably!) and proceeds go directly to the artists, and guest rooms feature local works by a rotating roster of nearly 70 artists. You don't even need to spend the night to peruse the works. Much like Tucson itself, the hotel welcomes anyone and everyone to experience the beauty of art.

Connect with...

㉕ Honor the dead at the All Souls Procession

㉖ Bike the Loop

㉝ See the mermaids on Fourth Avenue

29 Join La Fiesta de Los Vaqueros

Tucson Essential • Local Scenes

Why Go: One of the top 25 pro rodeos in the country, La Fiesta de Los Vaqueros halts business as usual in Tucson as the whole city comes out for this annual cowboy tradition.

Where: Tucson Rodeo Grounds • 4823 S. 6th Ave., Tucson, 520/741-2233, http://tucsonrodeo.com

Timing: This annual Professional Rodeo Cowboys Association (PRCA)-sanctioned event ($16-80 per person, $7 parking) takes place over nine days every February around Presidents' Day. The parade (free) hits the streets on Thursday at 9am, but you'll want to claim your spot on the route by 6am. Rodeo gates open daily at 11am. The Junior Rodeo starts at 12:30pm. The ProRodeo begins at 2pm and concludes at 4pm; the nightly barn dance kicks off shortly after that.

There's one thing you need to know about the rodeo: "Never don't pay attention."

It's an adage that holds weight for the fearless contestants and the rapt audience. Things happen in a flash—a horse bucks its rider, a steer outmaneuvers the loop of a rope—and if you take your eyes off the action for a second, you're left in the dust. Literally.

Arizona's "celebration of the cowboys," **La Fiesta de Los Vaqueros,** or more simply the Tucson Rodeo, started in 1925. It was the middle of Prohibition in a dusty frontier town, and organizers thought a rodeo would bring visitors eager for a glimpse of the Wild West. It worked. The first Tucson Rodeo, with its three days of events, was such a success that it evolved into a nine-day affair touted as one of the top 25 professional rodeos on the PRCA's calendar.

Here's what goes down: The sport's best cowboys and cowgirls compete in seven rodeo performances for prize money. The roughstock competitions include bareback riding, saddle bronc riding, and bull riding. The timed competitions feature steer wrestling, team roping, tie-down roping, and barrel racing.

All Tucson Rodeo events are open to the public. And let me tell you, the whole city

The crowd watches bull riders at the Tucson Rodeo.

Women's Barrel Racing competition

the swing of a lasso in the Team Roping event

Rodeo Through Serpa's Lens

Renowned rodeo photographer Louise Serpa coined that truism about paying attention. A New York City debutante turned tough-as-nails Western pioneer, Serpa photographed Tucson's esteemed La Fiesta de Los Vaqueros every year from 1963 to 2011. She was the first woman to be PRCA-sanctioned to shoot inside the arena, and for many years, she was the *only* woman to do so.

When she passed away in 2012 at the age of 86, she left behind a collection of some of the most vivid rodeo photography in the sport. Her images capture the grit and danger and athleticism of both human and animal—the muscular body of a bull arched in midair, a cowboy's tensed arm holding fast to the saddle—and show exactly why La Fiesta de Los Vaqueros is regarded as one of the most celebrated heritage events in the country.

shows up. School districts give students days off, businesses close early, and nearly 200,000 spectators line the streets to cheer on the Tucson Rodeo Parade, a two-mile line of horse-drawn floats and buggies, plus marching bands and Mexican folk dancers.

After each day's thrilling rodeo action—"after the last bull bucks," teases the invitation—everybody wipes the dirt from their boots and joins the Coors Barn Dance ($5 per person) to eat, drink, and two-step their way to the music of live bands.

The rodeo is one of those experiences that engages all of your senses: the sight of lunging, bucking bodies, the dank scent of animals, the clang of the bell and the crash of the gates, the foamy taste of cold beer, and a layer of dust so fine you'll find it on your skin for weeks. There's so much to take in. Just remember: "Never don't pay attention."

Connect with...

27 Outfit yourself in custom Western boots

30 Raise your glass at historic bars

32 Savor Sonoran-style food

30 Raise your glass at historic bars

Tucson Essential • Drink and Dine

Why Go: Raise a glass at these famous—and infamous—Tucson taverns, dive bars, and local watering holes.

Where: These historic bars are found throughout metro Tucson.

Timing: Most of these bars open in the afternoon and close between 2am and 3am. To feel like a neighborhood regular, show up when the bar first opens on a Tuesday or Wednesday. To see its rowdy side, show up around 10pm on a Saturday and stay until closing. For a relaxed vibe, show up on a Sunday morning for Bloody Marys.

The one and only time I've ever been to a bar before 9am (intentionally, that is) was in Tucson. To clarify, I'm talking about a *bar*. Not a coffee shop where you can get Bailey's in your latte. Not a swanky brunch place that also serves alcohol. I mean a bar—dark, boozy, probably old.

In this particular early-morning experience, "old" was the main draw; my husband and I were checking out **The Buffet Bar** (538 E. 9th St., 520/623-6811, www.thebuffetbar.com). Opened in 1934 just after Prohibition, The Buffet is Tucson's oldest drinking joint. It frequently tops bucket lists and "best of" roundups (including a few in *Esquire Magazine*) for reasons we hoped to uncover firsthand.

I expected a dive atmosphere, but I'd be lying if I didn't say that I thought its lowbrow aesthetic would be a little more, you know, curated. Like, divey in a movie-set kind of way. Nope. The Buffet Bar is the real deal, and thank goodness.

In a brick building in Tucson's historic Ironhorse 'hood, the bar's neon sign over the front door is probably the fanciest thing about the place. When we stepped inside, a few minutes passed before our eyes adjusted to the dimly lit interior. As the shadows retreated, we took in the lay of the land: a pool table in the corner, graffiti and art-tagged walls, Coors on tap, hot dogs simmering in a crockpot, and a bar anchoring the center of the room.

Most of the seats were occupied, even at this hour, and it seemed as though everyone

the classic signage at Hotel Congress

Buffet Bar, the oldest bar in Tucson

Pair a cocktail with some people-watching at Hotel Congress.

knew each other. After we sat and ordered our whiskey sours (heavy pour in a squat glass), it didn't take long to feel welcomed. A raised glass and a slight nod, and soon the regulars folded us into their banter. Strong drinks, easy conversation, and no pretense—that's how you keep a bar going for 87 years.

The Buffet Bar isn't the only revered pub in town with a long, decorated history, however. Tucson is home to several.

Though it's been around forever—opened in 1948, and in its current home since 1958— **Bay Horse Tavern** (2802 E. Grant Rd., 520/326-8554, https://bayhorsetavern.com) doesn't take itself too seriously. But it does offer everything you'd want in a bar: dart board, jukebox, solid cocktails, popcorn to snack on, and stools with seatbacks.

Since 1965, the **Golden Nugget Tavern** (2617 N. 1st Ave., 520/622-9202, www.goldennuggettucson.com) has been a favorite among drinkers who like things to do in between sips of their beer: pool tables, video games, shuffleboard, karaoke, televisions, and a loaded jukebox.

Keep the drinks simple at Tucson's old-school bars.

Honorable Mention

It can definitely be argued that **Hotel Congress** (311 E. Congress St., 520/622-8848, https://hotelcongress.com, 11am-11pm Sun.-Thurs., 11am-1am Fri.-Sat.) is one of the most historic hangouts in Tucson—thanks to its taproom opening date of 1919 and its infamy as the spot where John Dillinger was captured in 1934—but it's technically a hotel first, a bar second. Therefore: honorable mention.

Rivaling The Buffet Bar in age, **The Mint Bar** (3540 E. Grant Rd., 520/881-9169, www. themintbar.net) also opened in 1934. While bar patrons no longer ride their horses here, which local lore says they did well into the 1950s, they do enjoy The Mint's live music, Ping-Pong tables, and local craft beers on tap.

The Shelter Cocktail Lounge (4155 E. Grant Rd., 520/326-1345), a 1961 lounge, is a mid-century gem, frozen in time as Tucson's spot for martini swilling and go-go boot wearing. The drinks are expertly shaken, but even more impressive is The Shelter's retro decor: globe lights, red leather seats, and animal print wallpaper.

Don't get me wrong. I'm all for a mimosa at Sunday brunch or a post-work drink at the newest, hippest happy hour spot. But when you're looking for a place with character at which to raise a glass, always go for the bar that's a little bit dark and a lot weathered. Rule of thumb: The more lived in it feels, the more it's been loved.

Connect with...

28 Hunt for murals
33 See mermaids on Fourth Avenue

31 Summit "A" Mountain at sunrise

Tucson Essential • Outdoor Adventures • Beautiful Views

Why Go: Though known more as an iconic sunset spot, Tucson's "A" Mountain treats early risers to equally stunning sunrises, and with fewer crowds.

Where: Sentinel Peak Park • 1001 S. Sentinel Peak Rd., Tucson, 520/791-4873, www.tucsonaz.gov/parks/SentinelPeakPark

Timing: The vehicle gates (free admission) open daily at sunrise and close 30 minutes after sunset, year-round. To watch the sun as it's actually coming up (i.e., before the gates open), park in the lot at the bottom and walk Sentinel Peak Road (1.7 miles/2.7 km) to the top. Give yourself plenty of time before the sun starts peeking up over the eastern horizon.

As an Arizona State University (ASU) student, I spent many mornings hiking the short but steep ascent of Tempe's "A" Mountain at the north end of campus. Legs aching, heart racing, breath gasping, I climbed to where a gigantic gold-painted A—a proud nod to ASU—ornamented the peak for all to see. The view, especially at sunrise, was worth every tight muscle and accelerated heartbeat.

It was years later that I made a similar dawn expedition up the slopes of our state's other "A" Mountain: the prominence of **Sentinel Peak,** on the west side of downtown Tucson.

Here, in the Tucson Mountains, the giant basalt-rock A that rises in sharp relief on the slope stands not for ASU, but for the University of Arizona (UA). Students constructed it from 1914 to 1916 in celebration of a football win, hauling the 70-foot-wide, 160-foot-tall letter up the mountainside. The A is traditionally painted white, though over the years it's also sported other colors: black in protest of the Iraq War in 2003, green for St. Patrick's Day, blue to honor healthcare workers during the COVID-19 pandemic.

Sentinel Peak reaches nearly 2,900 feet high, and the Santa Cruz Valley ripples and undulates below. The fertile region—whose agricultural history dates back to 2000 BC—was first farmed by the Hohokam people. They grew crops along the Santa Cruz River, and the

See the landscape bathed in early morning light.

Hike early to enjoy the sunrise views.

bedrock mortars in Sentinel Peak Park are believed to have been used to grind corn and mesquite beans into flour. After the Hohokam people, the Tohono O'odham Nation, along with their close relatives the Akimel O'odham people (historically known as the Pima Indians), developed settlements throughout the Santa Cruz Valley.

It was the Tohono O'odham Nation who gifted Tucson its name, right here at Sentinel Peak. Because the base of the mountain—layered with igneous rock from volcanic activity—is darker than the summit, the Tohono O'odham named it Ts-iuk-shan, which means "the foot of the black hill." When the Spaniards arrived, they pronounced it Tuqui Son, or what we now call Tucson.

Summiting Sentinel Peak on foot is less of a trail hike and more of a paved walk. Sentinel Peak Road circles the mountain, and while it's not a difficult trek, it is a steady climb. Hundreds of people jog, walk, bike, and drive the route every day, but in the wee hours of the morning, you'll share the road with only a handful of other local rise-and-shiners.

As you wind around the mountain, note the remnants of ancient lava flows—a cluster of

the desert at sunrise from A Mountain

A Tale of Two "A"s

Because college rivals UA and ASU each boast an "A" Mountain, during the week leading up to the UA-ASU Territorial Cup football game, students from each team sneak up the opposing school's mountain (under the cover of night, of course) to paint the "A" in their own university colors.

outcroppings on the eastern edge—and how their erosion rounded the peak into its conical shape. Also keep an eye out for volcanic ash and lava beds. Come spring, these explode with wildflowers.

At the peak, 360-degree views greet you. Find an east-facing boulder on which to stretch your legs and calm your beating heart. Then take in the sight of a pink- and purple-saturated sky, saguaros in silhouette, and Tucson—Ts-iuk-shan—curled up at the mountain's base.

Connect with...

26 Bike the Loop

28 Hunt for murals

41 Enjoy desert blooms and autumn leaves

32 Savor Sonoran-style food

Drink and Dine • Local Scenes

Why Go: The hot, dry, and surprisingly bountiful landscape of the Sonoran Desert has been influencing the region's cuisine for hundreds of years, resulting in foods that are truly unique to this part of the world.

Where: Though Sonoran cuisine can be found all over Arizona, these restaurants are located in metro Tucson.

Timing: A handheld tamale is built to be gobbled on the go. But I'm a fan of a long, leisurely meal, so plan to spend an hour or two to indulge. Most of the places suggested here are family-operated, so take time to chat with the owners, ask questions about the menu, and sample ingredients you've never tried.

Sonoran-style fare is rooted in the cooking styles of the people of Sonora, Mexico, and in the ingredients grown in the Sonoran Desert, which stretches from northwestern Mexico into the United States, encompassing both Phoenix and Tucson. Sonoran food aligns closely with Mexican food (think tortillas, beans, and rice), with a major distinction being the use of flour. Wheat grows well here, so unlike Tex-Mex, New Mexican, or Baja cuisine, Sonoran food favors flour tortillas over corn. A few other Sonoran hallmarks: beef (*carne asada* and *machaca*, thanks to the many cattle ranches), cactus (the pads and the fruit), sweet agave, flat (never rolled) enchiladas, chiles (such as the native *chiltepin*), mesquite (for smoked meats and baking flour), tepary beans, and salsas.

There's not one single neighborhood—or even city—in Arizona that lays sole claim to Sonoran-style cuisine: You can find it throughout the state, from Nogales to Tucson and Phoenix, even all the way to Flagstaff. I recommend sampling as much Sonoran-style fare in as many places as possible, but if you want to stick to just one locale, here are my favorites in Tucson.

The tamales at **Tucson Tamale Company** (7159 E. Tanque Verde, 520/298-8404, and 7286 N. Oracle Rd., 520/403-1888, https://market.tucsontamale.com) are hand-wrapped in

▲ a mural by Lalo Cota outside of Barrio Café in Phoenix

▲ tamale

▲ Sonoran hot dog

photos of the original Carolina's line the walls of the restaurant

corn husks and stuffed with ingredients such as green and red chiles, pork, beef, blue corn, black beans—even pumpkin. A traditional holiday meal, tamales can be eaten for breakfast, lunch, or dinner. The tamales at Tucson Tamale Company are so good that many Tucson markets, coffee shops, bars, and festivals bring in big hauls to sell individually. If you see a place offering them, don't hesitate. Buy immediately. You can also order directly from Tucson Tamales; they'll ship anywhere.

Chef Maria Mazon is a master in the kitchen of her Tucson restaurant, **Boca Tacos y Tequila** (533 N. 4th Ave., 520/777-8134, https://bocatacos.com). She was born in Tucson but grew up in Sonora, Mexico, and her innovative dishes reflect both countries as well as the Sonoran Desert that blankets the region. Her flair for the experimental shows up in her original salsas, which she often names after friends and family. Chef Maria makes them in-house at her bustling restaurant near the University of Arizona campus using chiles, mesquite-smoked whiskeys, and anything else she can get her hands on.

Then there's the Sonoran hot dog, one of those only-in-Arizona delicacies. When vis-

Also in Phoenix

Manuel and Carolina Valenzuela began selling homemade tortillas out of their car in the 1950s. Now the family operates the successful brick-and-mortar **Carolina's Mexican Restaurant** (2126 E. Cactus Rd., Phoenix, 602/275-8231, www.carolinasmexicanfood. com). Here, people line up for a stack of freshly made tortillas—giant flour disks that come off the grill warm, tender, and thin. And though Mexican law says tequila can only be produced in Jalisco, there are those of us who consider a *reposado* tequila to be an important part of a Sonoran meal. **Barrio Café** (2814 N. 16th St., Phoenix, 602/636-0240, www.barriocafe.com) offers more than 200 tequilas, from bright silver to aged añejo. Admittedly, the menu from James Beard Award nominee Silvana Salcido Esparza leans Central Mexican, but almost every dish is laced with Sonoran chiles—poblano, serrano, and jalapeño. When she's not in the kitchen, you might see Chef Silvana driving around the restaurant's neighborhood—*"mi barrio,"* as she calls it—in a custom low-rider.

itors come to town, this is the dish I foist on them: a bacon-wrapped hot dog topped with beans, tomatoes, onions, mushrooms, and mayonnaise, all on a steamy, soft bun. You'll mostly find the Sonoran hot dog at food trucks roving around Tucson; they'll post up in a parking lot with an awning or tent shading folding tables where customers eat. The first one I ever had was from **El Sinaloense Hot Dog Cart** (1526 N. Alvernon Way, 520/358-0779) in Tucson, and it still reigns supreme to me.

The best part about a regional food expedition is there's always something new (to you) to try, or a surprising iteration of a traditional favorite. Once you embark on a tasting tour of Sonoran-style fare, I guarantee you'll never want to stop.

Connect with...

24 Taste Tucson's global flavors
25 Honor the dead at the All Souls Procession
34 Stroll the Heirloom Farmers Market at Rillito Park

33 See the mermaids on Fourth Avenue

Tucson Essential • Fun for Families and Kids • Local Scenes

Why Go: This is your chance to see mermaids and mermen in the desert! Plus costume contests, live music, kids' games, art installations, and good food from favorite Tucson eateries.

Where: Events take place along Fourth Avenue • https://fourthavenue.org/return-of-the-mermaids

Timing: This festival packs a lot of activity into one summer day, usually the second Saturday of August. Most events kick off at 2pm. Family-friendly fun runs until about 8pm; from 9pm to 2am, you'll find activities for the 21 and older crowd. Vendors and venues are set up all along Fourth Avenue, so be prepared to walk about a mile or so.

In Phoenix and Tucson, monsoon season brings a brief respite from the scalding summer heat. In July and August, afternoon clouds gather dark and swollen in the sky, ready to unleash torrents of rain, quick slivers of lightning, and booms of thunder. These monsoon storms end as abruptly as they begin—always too short, yet leaving us desperately grateful for the cooler temperatures and sun coverage. It's here, in the dry and parched desert, that you'll find a full-fledged festival celebrating the storms of the monsoon. Let me introduce you to **Return of the Mermaids.**

Hosted by Historic Fourth Avenue, this party—weird, whimsical, wonderful—converges on downtown Tucson and invites all merfolk, from mermaids to mermen and merkids, to dive into the legend and lore of the ocean. Since 2013, the festival has attracted nearly 15,000 people.

The festival's mythology goes something like this: During the season when the rain soaks the thirsty earth, water penetrates the cracks in the hard ground. As it seeps through the dirt, it awakens the undersea creatures living deep below the surface of Tucson, who then emerge, gracing us with their presence for one day only.

Who are these mystical creatures? You can meet them when they make their appear-

Watch the mermaids celebrate monsoon season.

Kid-friendly events abound at the Return of the Mermaids festival.

mermaid

Meet the Mermaids

The festival features several professional mermaids. Tucson's veteran mermaid is Emy Higdon. She's been in character as Mermaid Odette for more than a decade. Arizona native Michelle Mozdzen, aka Mermaid Michelle, lawyers by day and mermaids on the side. Michelle Ruffo, or Mermaid Michelina, has been mermaiding for nearly 10 years.

ance at Return of the Mermaids' live aquarium—a reef where merfolks mesmerize the crowds with songs, games, even wish-granting—and at photo ops throughout the festival.

Nearly 20 more events comprise the celebration, including a treasure hunt, kids dance party, and sea-inspired art installations. Looking for synchronized swimming? Check. How about an ocean-themed circus-arts parade? Check. Face painting and glitter tattoos? Check and check. You'll also find a beach, a pirate ship, and an artisan market hosted by local Tucson makers and the independently owned shops that Fourth Avenue is famous for.

Attendees are highly encouraged to don their best mermaid and merman attire, all of which are on sparkly display at all-ages costume contests, a children's sidewalk parade, a mermaid pageant, and "sealife" performances. For those of us who don't have a go-to merfolk outfit hanging in the closet, or perhaps aren't into cosplay, think of it like this: It's 120 degrees outside and you're probably already wearing a swimsuit anyway. What's a few sequins and some green hair dye?

I'll be honest. When I first heard about Return of the Mermaids, I didn't get it. We live in the Sonoran Desert, more than 400 miles from the Pacific Ocean. Our lakes are human-made. Our riverbeds run dry. And yet. It seems to be this very absence of water that makes us hold it so dear, that means those flash storms are all the more treasured.

Connect with...

29 Join La Fiesta de Los Vaqueros
30 Raise your glass at historic bars
32 Savor Sonoran-style food

34 Stroll the Heirloom Farmers Market at Rillito Park

Fun for Families and Kids • Drink and Dine • Shopping

Why Go: All the very best things about Tucson—international culinary flavors, a neighborly sense of community, lazy Sundays in a laid-back city—are rounded up in one happy place.

Where: 4502 N. 1st Ave., Tucson, 520/882-2157, www.heirloomfm.org/markets/rilli-to-park

Timing: The farmers market at Rillito Park is one of five Heirloom Farmers Markets in the region, each open on a different day. The market at Rillito Park is open every Sunday. From October to April, it runs 9am-1pm; from April 16 to September, it runs 8am-noon. If you have your eye on certain produce or goodies known to sell out, arrive early to nab your stash.

On a recent Sunday morning—with the sun beaming warm but the air still cool—at the **Heirloom Farmers Market at Rillito Park,** a woman eyed a crate of ripe tomatoes. The globes of fruit at the Tomato Family stand, a seasonal vendor that sells homegrown greenhouse tomatoes, sported shades of yellow, orange, and green. The woman picked them up, one at a time, and examined each closely. Finally, she settled on two plump green ones. She handed over a wad of cash, tucked the tomatoes in her tote, and threaded her way through the crowd to join the line at **Adventure Coffee Roasting.**

I watched another woman walk her leashed labrador past the colorful tarts and flaky croissants of **Café Francais** while a young couple learned all about the naturopathic benefits of elderberry from the **Prickly Paradise Elderberry** stand. Before they moved on, I saw them purchase a small brown bag labeled "Elderberry Syrup Kit."

Who were these moseyers and browsers and shoppers? Where were they off to next, I wondered? Who knows? They probably couldn't even say. And that's the magic of the Rillito Farmers Market, Tucson's largest year-round farmers market. It's a giant gastronomy gathering—complete with 5,000 square feet, four pavilions, and a live entertainment space—of southern Arizona's farmers, ranchers, and artisan food purveyors. They meet and greet, they

Crowds browse the goods at the Rillito Farmers Market.

fresh produce at Rillito Farmers Market

set up their booths, and they sell their fresh-as-can-be goods to locals. And guests? They wander, following their inner compass of desire and interest.

A few market vendor standouts include **Mustang Mountain Eggs** from Huachuca City and **Zamudio Eggs** from Elfrida; the **Jojoba Beef Company** and their free-grazing cattle; the organic honey, honeycomb, bee pollen, skin cream, and beeswax candles from **Terry's Apiaries;** the homemade pupusas and tamales from **Selena's Salvadorian Food;** dried nuts, fruit, and seeds from **High Country Nuts; Green Heart Bakery's** vegan pastries; and the award-winning cheese (chevre, feta, ricotta, soft ripened) from **Fiore Di Capra Goat Cheese.**

The Rillito Farmers Market is more than just fresh fare and good produce. As an organization, the Heirloom Farmers Market values sustainability and supporting local business. Red "Get Real Certification" tags at vendor booths indicate farmers who are growing and producing their food locally. The organization has also teamed up with Living Streets Alliance to encourage bicycle travel to the market with an annual event, appropriately titled

⌃ basket full of okra

Shopping Tips

If you've never done the farmers market thing, your first trip can be overwhelming. Here are a few tips courtesy of Heirloom Farmers Markets: Shop early, bring cash, wear comfortable shoes, bring your own bags, and write a grocery list before you leave the house. But also be open to making a surprise purchase—going off-book is the best part of farmers market shopping!

"Bike to the Farmers Market." Because the Rillito Farmers Market is situated on Tucson's citywide, 130+-mile (209-km) bicycle trail, **The Loop,** it makes perfect sense to inspire Tucsonans to get to the market on two wheels.

At the market, look for quarterly food demonstrations, seasonal food festivals, and local live music. Talk to the vendors. Ask questions. Make new friends. Or just do what I do. Grab a mesquite-flour baked pastry from **Big Skye Bakers,** sit back, and soak up the excellent people-watching.

Connect with...

24 Taste Tucson's global flavors
26 Bike the Loop
32 Savor Sonoran-style food

35 Transform your backyard with desert plants

Why Go: Arid-happy plants native to Arizona are some of the most interesting and unique flora in nature, and they offer a wonderful way to beautify your home landscape sustainably.

Where: Tohono Chul • 7366 Paseo del Norte, Tucson, 520/742-6455, www.downtowntempe.com/go/tempe-town-lake

Timing: The grounds are open 8am-5pm daily, the shop and galleries are open 9am-5pm daily, and the restaurant is open 8am-3pm Wednesday-Sunday. The spring plant sale happens in March, the fall plant sale takes place in November, and the summer "monsoon madness" sale occurs every July. Admission costs $15 for adults, $13 for seniors, military, and students, $6 for children ages 5-12, and is free for children younger than 5.

A few years ago a friend showed up at my house bearing a surprise gift. It was a teacup-sized plastic planter with a green stub of bark, carrot-y in shape, sprouting from the dirt. It bloomed no flowers, it boasted no delicate branches, it sported no leaves save for two—small, like thumbnails—that stuck out from a nub on the side of its trunk. It was the ugliest plant I'd ever seen. I loved it.

The *Adenium arabicum*, aka "desert rose," aka "fat guy," is a bulbous succulent that can grow up to 10 feet tall. It does eventually flower too, I learned later. The hardy plant requires little water and lots of sunlight, which makes it perfect for desert living. My sweet friend bought my fella at Phoenix's Desert Botanical Garden (she also got one for herself), but the *Adenium arabicum* is exactly the kind of plant you'll find at **Tohono Chul** in Tucson.

The 49-acre botanical garden slash art gallery slash plant store shares its mission of connecting people to the nature, art, and culture of the Sonoran Desert while also inspiring stewardship of our natural lands. Designed to attract wildlife (especially hummingbirds and butterflies), the park's themed gardens use native and arid-adapted plants to showcase the diversity of habitats in the Sonoran Desert.

Wander the courtyard of Tohono Chul.

Adenium arabicum, or desert rose

A window overlooks the beautiful grounds of Tohono Chul.

A stroll along the walking paths might treat you to a desert palm canyon rich with rock fig, sea grape, and jasmine, and a stream that's home to endangered native fish; or a seasonal garden with ironwood, desert willow, and my favorite cactus, the ocotillo; or a field full of drought-tolerant, wildlife-friendly, bright and colorful penstemon flowers. And throughout, engaging educational opportunities—from workshops and lectures to guided tours and informational signage—abound, giving you a chance to take a deep dive into anything and everything related to Sonoran Desert plant life.

Whether you spend 30 minutes or three hours here, inspiration to re-create Tohono Chul's natural beauty for your own outdoor spaces will strike. When this happens, head to the park's **Retail Greenhouse.**

In this soaring, sunlit, glass-enclosed room, you'll find tables crowded with native cactuses, shelves lined with leafy arid-adapted plants, and rows and rows of succulents, wildflowers, grasses, and spiky agave. Wander and browse, then alight on any one of Tohono

▲ the grounds of Tohono Chul

Table for Two

With some of the best views of the Santa Catalina Mountains, the park's bistro is a favorite local spot for regionally inspired breakfast, brunch, and lunch. Don't miss the prickly pear margarita, a summer drink made with harvested fruit.

Chul's staff members. The park's green-thumb experts are on hand to answer questions and guide you through the ins and outs of how to plant a desert-friendly backyard oasis.

Tohono Chul collects seeds from the plants growing in the park's gardens, and they also buy seeds from native seed collectors to propagate the flora available for purchase in the greenhouse. Three times a year (March, July, and November) the park hosts a plant sale where you can discover odd, beautiful, and unique cold-hardy plants not found anywhere else. And hey, maybe if you're lucky, you just might stumble upon your very own ugly-but-lovable *Adenium arabicum* to take home.

Connect with...

24 Taste Tucson's global flavors
34 Stroll the Heirloom Farmers Market at Rillito Park
41 Enjoy desert blooms and autumn leaves

36 **See wild horses along the Salt River**

Outdoor Adventures • Fun for Families and Kids • Beautiful Views

Why Go: Untamed, unclaimed, and wild, majestic horses roam the Lower Salt River in the Tonto National Forest, embodying the very spirit of the American West.

Where: Lower Salt River, Mesa, 480/868-9301, https://saltriverwildhorsemanagementgroup.org

Timing: The horses live in the Tonto National Forest, strolling down to the Salt River to quench their thirst. For this reason, the best time of year to see them is when the Salt River's water levels are highest, mid-May through mid-October. Aim for dusk or dawn. A Tonto pass ($8, available online at www.fs.usda.gov/detail/tonto/passes-permits and at nearby gas stations) is required to park along the Salt River.

My husband and I had to put our kayaks in at Water Users Recreation Site, hauling them through the scrub brush to the banks of the river. Then we were idly paddling. No whitewater rapids to strong-arm here. Snaking 200 miles through the Tonto National Forest, the Salt River may be the largest tributary of the Gila River, but its waters run more like a generous creek than a powerful river.

As we drifted downstream, I dipped my paddle in the river sporadically—to gently shove the boat off a rock or spoon cooling water on my legs. The summer day had been hot, the sun relentless. Thankfully dusk was near. We planned to kayak to Coon Bluff Campground, which would get us out of the river after sunset but before dark.

It was then, somewhere between Blue Point and Coon Bluff, that I heard it. Rustling in the grass, shaking branches in the mesquite forest, and a thunderous pounding. Suddenly, they burst through the trees. A herd of wild horses.

I'd heard of the famous horses on the Outer Banks of North Carolina, and in my home state of Maryland, more than 300 wild horses live on Assateague Island. But until this moment, I'd never seen such a thing myself.

In front of me were eight horses, their muscular bodies in silky shades of brown and

See the horses run and frolic together.

The horses cool off in the Salt River.

⌃ Salt River wild horses

white and gray. They splashed into the river and clip-clopped over the rocks, stopping to drink or munch on eelgrass. We stayed as still as we could in our kayaks. My phone was, of course, zipped up in a watertight case inside the hull of the boat. I didn't dare move to grab it. This breathtaking moment would have to be immortalized in my mind.

I learned later that these wild horses have been living, playing, and roaming on the Lower Salt River for centuries. It's believed that the present-day herds descended from horses brought to the Southwest in the 1600s by Spanish missionary Father Eusebio Kino. The **Salt River Wild Horse Management Group** (SRWHMG), which maintains the humane stewardship of the horses today, found early evidence of their existence in an article from 1890. It classified the Salt River horses as "native stock," a classification that can only be given if at least five generations of people know about them.

I'll never forget that day in the kayaks. Two horses—one with an ebony mane, the other smaller, lighter, with a spotted coat—peeled off from the group to wade into the river. The waves lapped at their chests and their tails whisked madly. Soon the rest of the horses fol-

Save the Horses

The horses faced forced removal as recently as 2015. But thanks to public outcry and the efforts of SRWHMG, the horses are now protected under federal and state laws. Not only are they left to live peacefully, but SRWHMG also monitors them, keeping records of each horse, rescuing critically injured horses, and operating an emergency response program that includes feedings during severe droughts.

To help these precious and endangered creatures, consider volunteering with the SRWHMG. From monitoring horses on the river to mucking stalls at the group's horse sanctuary, you can assist in myriad ways. No experience necessary, just keep one day a week free to dedicate to the cause.

lowed, and then the herd cantered away from us, back into the trees. And just like that, they were gone.

For a chance to see the horses for yourself, stop by the **Blue Point Recreation Area** (www.fs.usda.gov/recarea/tonto/recarea/?recid=35405), **Coon Bluff Campground** (www.fs.usda.gov/recarea/tonto/null/recarea/?recid=35399&actid=31), or **Goldfield Recreation Area** (www.fs.usda.gov/recarea/tonto/null/recarea?recid=35403&actid=34).

Connect with...

⑩ Stretch out at goat yoga
㊶ Enjoy desert blooms and autumn leaves
㊼ Join a star party

37 Helicopter over the world's fourth-tallest fountain

Beautiful Views • Fun for Families and Kids • Outdoor Adventures

Why Go: Fountain Hills is one of the metro area's prettiest enclaves, and there's nothing quite like seeing its sweep of emerald-green golf courses, azure-blue pools, and famous sparkling fountain from the seat of a helicopter.

Where: 360 Adventures • 480/722-0360, www.360-adventures.com

Timing: Air tours ($400/solo adult, $250/adult for 2 or more guests, $200/children ages 2-9; reservations required) are available year-round, weather dependent. Flights depart from Scottsdale Airpark (15000 N. Airport Dr., Scottsdale, 480/312-2321, www.scottsdaleaz.gov/airport). Flight duration is 30 minutes; plan to be at the airport 30 minutes before takeoff.

That Fountain Hills was designed by one of the chief developers of Disneyland explains a lot about the 12,000-acre planned community. The manicured aesthetic, for one. Pristine streets ribboning through dewy golf courses and past glass-walled mansions, and a downtown hub fashioned after Main Street USA. For two, the spectacle that is the centerpiece of the town: a sparkling lake in the middle of the desert from which a towering plume of water bursts forth every hour on the hour.

This isn't just any fountain, of course. As a town styled after a very particular vision, Fountain Hills' watery icon needed to make a statement. And it does. Most days the fountain splashes up from its concrete water-lily bed to an impressive 330 feet, but at its full height, it rises 560 feet. To put that into perspective, 560 feet is three times higher than the height of Old Faithful in Yellowstone National Park, 110 feet higher than the Great Pyramid of Giza in Egypt, taller than Notre Dame in Paris, and taller than the Washington Monument. This puts Fountain Hills on the map as home to one of the tallest fountains in the world.

The fountain runs daily from 9am to 9pm, shimmering into a tower of water for 15 minutes before receding back into the lake. The spectacle can be seen for miles around, from Carefree to the Superstition Mountains. But for epic viewing, join a helicopter tour

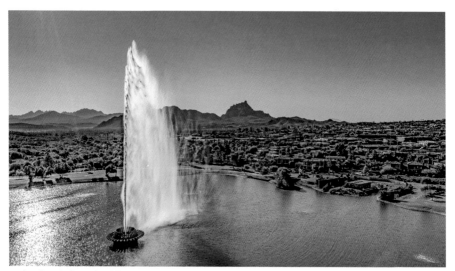

the gigantic fountain of Fountain Hills

Green golf courses envelop Fountain Hills.

of Fountain Hills piloted by 360 Adventures. The Arizona-based company hosts all manner of guided thrills, such as canyoneering in Globe, rock climbing at Papago Park, kayaking at Saguaro Lake, plus cycling, hiking, and ballooning. During Cactus League Spring Training, 360 Adventures even offers helicopter rides over the city's spring training baseball stadiums on game days (from $795/flight, tours run 45-90 minutes).

Among the company's helicopter flights, the half-hour Fountain Hills tour is a great way to see not just Fountain Hills, but also the neighborhoods in and around the middle of metro Phoenix.

The trip starts in Scottsdale, and then soars over Paradise Valley and the crags of Piestewa Peak. It buzzes around Camelback Mountain before ducking east through the McDowell Mountains and over Fountain Hills. The pilot slash tour guide shares stories of intrigue about the ghost towns and outlaw hideouts of the Superstitions, facts about regional wildlife and unique geographical features, and history of the community, such as how it was first

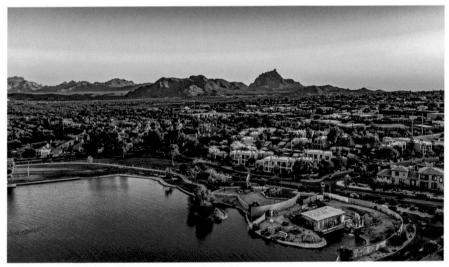

The streets of Fountain Hills curve around the town's lake.

Did You Know?

Even though Fountain Hills is part of the fifth-largest city in the nation, it's surrounded by the McDowell Mountains, which screen the community from the never-ending glow of city lights. Fountain Hills enjoys surprisingly dark nights and has taken efforts to preserve its starry skies; in 2018 the town earned an official designation as an **International Dark Sky Community.**

established by cattlemen in the 1800s or how the land was bought in 1970 and officially incorporated as Fountain Hills in 1989.

An aerial tour of Fountain Hills shows off all the thoughtful details and intricate layouts of a planned community. It's like flying over a dollhouse village or a storybook diorama. You might be tempted to make a Stepford joke or two until you see just how pretty and picturesque and perfect it is—like Disneyland, where make-believe creates real magic.

Connect with...

❶ Take to the sky in a hot-air balloon
⓬ Play hooky at a Cactus League Spring Training game
㊿ Join a star party

38 Dine in the desert

Drink and Dine • Beautiful Views • Outdoor Adventures

Why Go: These culinary events are about more than just great food (although that's certainly a worthy reason to book a reservation). They whisk you away to unexpected places, foster friendships, inspire community, and help conserve the state's natural lands.

Where: Dinners are held at various remote locations throughout Arizona, 480/428-6028, https://clothandflame.com

Timing: Most dinners start at 5:30pm and conclude between 10pm and 11pm. Because the events tend to be located in remote places on the outskirts of urban areas, accessible only by back roads, plan for an additional two hours of driving (round-trip). Attendees must be 21 years of age or older.

The first thing I noticed was the dining table. Long, elegantly plated, bunches of wildflowers poking out of glass jars, string lights dangling, surrounded on all sides by nature.

An Instagram story come to life? Or a desert mirage?

We'd jostled along a bumpy dirt road into the Superstition Wilderness, and just when I thought we'd never again see another soul, a clearing emerged among the mesquite trees and there it was. A table, set for a group of strangers to break bread under the sky. I'd hiked this area many times, a rugged part of the Sonoran Desert, where a squished granola bar in my backpack was the height of gastronomy.

That community table was no mirage. I was attending a **Cloth & Flame** dinner, a multi-course adventure in the middle of nowhere. When I first bought my ticket (from $145 per person), I didn't know what to expect. Phoenix-based owners Matt Cooley and Olivia Laux described it as an immersive wilderness dining experience.

What this means (as I came to find out later): The couple leases Arizona land in forests, canyons, and deserts, along creeks and cliffsides, among red rocks and hoodoos, then sets up a table and invites a notable chef to wield their culinary powers.

For foodies, an evening with Cloth & Flame is a dream come true. Local ingredients star,

Make new friends over a desert dinner.

Conserving Arizona's Wild Lands

A few of the organizations to which Cloth & Flame have donated funds include Arizona State Parks, Superstition Area Land Trust, the Sonoran Institute, and Last Prisoner Project, a nonprofit organization focused on cannabis criminal justice reform.

and courses are paired with stellar wines, beers, or cocktails. As the dishes keep coming and the booze keeps flowing, strangers become friends. It's magic.

Cloth & Flame dinners have featured the likes of James Beard Award-winner Chris Bianco of **Pizzeria Bianco** (623 E. Adams St., Phoenix, 602/258-8300, and 4743 N. 20th St., Phoenix, 602/368-3273; www.pizzeriabianco.com) and acclaimed chef Pornsupak "Cat" Bunnag of **Glai Baan** (2333 E. Osborn Rd., Phoenix, 602/595-5881, www.glaibaanaz.com). They've brought in craft brewers, such as **Arizona Wilderness** (201 E. Roosevelt St., Phoe-

Cloth & Flame owners Matt Cooley and Olivia Laux

nix, 480/462-1836, and 721 N. Arizona Ave. #103, Gilbert, 480/497-2739; https://azwbeer. com), and local mezcal maker **Mezcal Carreño** (https://mezcalcarrenous.com).

Dinners have taken place on the banks of Oak Creek in Sedona, in the sprawling desert near Lake Pleasant, at Saguaro National Park in Tucson, even perched on the side of the Grand Canyon.

The food is incredible. The menu at a recent cannabis-infused dining experience in the Verde Valley showcased a starter of peaches, beets, and feta, followed by orecchiette with summer squash and cannabis pesto, then achiote-crusted pork with blackberry mole, concluded by horchata ice cream and toasted pecans.

Perhaps even more satisfying than the food is the fact that Cooley and Laux put the proceeds from ticket sales toward a good cause. Not only does Cloth & Flame pay the property owner a venue fee for hosting—therefore helping to economically sustain lands that might otherwise be developed—but the company also donates an additional 10 percent to a nonprofit dedicated to land preservation and the conservation of migratory routes. Cloth & Flame's table-to-desert approach is all about awareness, showing people that untouched wilderness areas exist and are worth saving.

Connect with...

6 Toast an Arizona brew
18 Watch the sun set at South Mountain Park
24 Taste Tucson's global flavors

39 Dip into hot springs

Why Go: A soothing soak in one of Arizona's myriad hot springs brings body and mind rejuvenation with healing powers of stress relief, better blood circulation, and plenty of get-away-from-it-all natural beauty.

Where: Arizona Hot Spring, 702/293-8990, www.nps.gov/lake/planyourvisit/hikeazhot.htm • Kaiser Hot Springs • Verde River Hot Springs, www.paysonrimcountry.com/verde-hot-river-springs

Timing: There aren't many things more satisfying than soaking in a therapeutic hot tub when the ambient temperature is chilly. Hence why I recommend a visit to Arizona's hot springs during the cooler months of late fall, winter, or early spring. Most of these geothermal pools are open year-round, though, so when the need for a wellness retreat arises—no matter the season—heed the call.

Many places in the United States, especially in the West, claim their share of hot springs. Arizona is no exception.

The springs are warmed by heat from the earth's interior, known as geothermal heat. In volcanic areas, water mixes with hot magma rock. If that water soaks deeply enough into the crust, it connects with hot rocks and bubbles up to the surface of the earth to form hot springs and cozy soaking pools.

Archaeological evidence traces Native peoples' use of the springs back 10,000 years. In Arizona, the American Indians considered the springs sacred because of what they believed to be the healing powers of the water's intense heat and high mineral content.

Things aren't so different today—hot-springs seekers scale rock faces, hike into slot canyons, and tiptoe along cliff edges to reach these natural watering holes.

The once-famous-but-now-primitive **Verde River Hot Springs** (free) sits on the western edge of the Verde River southeast of Camp Verde. Near the large soaking pool rest the ruins of a former mid-century wellness resort and bathhouse. The 2.5 mile (4 km) out-and-back trail to the springs is moderate. It's a hike that's vigorous enough to make you feel

Half the fun of Arizona Hot Spring is the hike to get there.

Castle Hot Springs offers resort amenities with a hot springs soak.

▲ trail to Arizona Hot Spring

like the journey was worth it, but not so demanding that you're depleted when you finally emerge at the tranquil spot. Note: The springs aren't the hottest—temperatures reach about 98 degrees F—but the picturesque setting eases all tensions. To get there from Camp Verde, head east on AZ 260 for 7 miles (11 km). Turn right onto Forest Road 708/Fossil Creek Road. Continue for 15 miles (24 km) until you reach the junction of Forest Road 708 and Forest Road 502. Take Forest Road 502 south for 6 miles (10 km).

Jagged rock walls rise high around **Kaiser Hot Springs** (free), located between King-man and Wickenburg. The shallow pool warms up to about 100 degrees F and tucks into Warm Springs Canyon, a short slot canyon that arrows through saguaro and cholla cactuses. If you follow the sandy wash through the canyon, you'll reach Burro Creek, a great swim-ming hole in its own right. To find Kaiser, drive 62 miles (100 km) northwest of Wickenburg on US 93. Exit at Burro Creek Bridge and park in the area on the east side. From here you can access the trailhead, following signs for the Kaiser Spring Wash.

To reach the secluded **Arizona Hot Spring** at Lake Mead Recreation Area ($25 per

City Slickers

A hot-springs soak doesn't have to involve a high-clearance vehicle and a remote wilderness adventure. At **Castle Hot Springs** (5050 E. Castle Hot Springs Rd., Morristown, 877/600-1137, www.castlehotsprings.com), you can relax in the hottest non-volcanic spring in the world, luxury-style. The resort's hot-spring pools and VIP guest treatment attract elite travelers from all over the world.

vehicle, entrance valid for 7 days), you'll hike about 5 miles (8 km) round-trip from the trailhead off US 93 (8 mi/13 km from the Lake Mead Visitor Center) into a narrow slot canyon near the Colorado River. The springs are nice and hot, topping out at about 110 degrees F, and they neighbor a cascading 20-foot waterfall. Take the White Rock Canyon trail through a ravine, past volcanic rock, and along the shores of Lake Mohave. Once you reach the slot canyon, look for the ladder that leads you to the springs.

Connect with...

43 Go wine-tasting
45 Haunt a ghost town
48 Drive the Joshua Tree Parkway

40 **Backpack the backcountry**

Outdoor Adventures • Weekend Getaways

Why Go: Living in Phoenix or Tucson, you're within 90 minutes of millions of acres of diverse wildlife and rich ecosystems. A backcountry excursion is the way to immerse yourself in our state's impressive natural landscapes.

Where: Visit Mount Wrightson, Sycamore Canyon, the Superstition Wilderness, and Homolovi State Park for great backpacking opportunities.

Timing: Plan 3-5 days for a backpacking trip. This includes driving time to and from the trailheads. If you're backpacking point to point, make sure you've made pick-up arrangements. Seasonality depends on where you're going. Winter and spring are ideal for southern and central Arizona trips, while summer and fall are perfect for northern Arizona adventures.

I'm outdoorsy. But I'm not *outdoorsy* outdoorsy. At least I wasn't until I learned a few fascinating facts about Arizona's backcountry.

One: Arizona ranks second in the nation for states with the most federally designated wilderness areas (we have 90). Two: The state possesses 4.5 million acres of pristine natural lands. And three: All this land is open for safe exploration. So I bought sturdy hiking boots, a headlamp, and a backpack the size of a Labrador retriever. Then I hit the trails.

Backpacking isn't for everyone, but with a little preparation and a sense of adventure, you can find a multiday trail that suits your comfort and skill levels.

South of Tucson, the difficult but breathtaking 13.1-mile (21-km) **Mount Wrightson Loop Trail** (Tucson, www.fs.usda.gov/main/coronado/home) switchbacks through the lush Santa Rita Mountains on its route to the peak of Mount Wrightson, which sits at nearly 9,500 feet. As part of the loop, there's the challenging Old Baldy Trail as well as the (slightly) easier—and more isolated—Super Trail. Drive south from Tucson on I-19 to the Continental Road/Madera Canyon exit. Go east, following Madera Canyon signs to the trailhead at Bog Springs Campground.

For something shorter and less strenuous, head to Flagstaff for the 7.3-mile (11.7-km)

Mount Wrightson

Kelsey-Dorsey Loop (www.fs.usda.gov/coconino). The most difficult part of this trek will be the rugged drive to the trailhead along Forest Road (FR) 231. Because a high-clearance vehicle is needed to navigate the terrain, crowds and cars are few. Hike the loop through Douglas firs, ponderosa pines, junipers, and oaks, with stops at several natural springs. The hike never traverses Sycamore Canyon, but it does grant stunning views of it. From Route 66, take FR 231 for 20 miles (32 km) to the trailhead.

Ready for an epic 23-mile (37-km) round-trip quest in the Sonoran Desert? Then hit up **White Rock Springs** (www.fs.usda.gov/main/tonto/home). Just on the outskirts of Phoenix near Apache Junction, this moderately difficult multiday hike threads through the Superstition Wilderness and all of its wild glory: rocky hills and towering boulders, saguaros and cholla, remote campsites, and very few people. Start at First Water Trailhead and plan for three days and two nights for this trip. Pack a GPS and a good map, as well as plenty of water (three liters per person).

Wheelchair-accessible backcountry trails can be found throughout the state, especially

▲ the red rocks of Sedona

Backpacking Safety

Exploring remote backcountry can be challenging. Be honest about your physical abilities and backpacking prowess. And no matter your skill level, always be prepared. Contact **REI Adventure Center Arizona** (866-455-1601, https://destinations.rei.com/arizona) for gear rentals, guide-led excursions, outdoors preparedness classes, packing lists, and maps. To check water availability—real-time stream flow, groundwater, and water quality—use the online **USGS National Water Dashboard** (www.usgs.gov/centers/az-water). For information on trail conditions, seasonal closures, and weather, contact **Arizona Bureau of Land Management** (602-417-9200, www.blm.gov/arizona) or the **U.S. Forest Service** (www.fs.usda.gov).

at many of the **Arizona State Parks** (https://azstateparks.com). **Homolovi State Park** (I-40, exit 257, 928/289-4106, https://azstateparks.com/homolovi) near Winslow offers a 0.5-mile (0.8-km) trail leading to a well-preserved Native archaeological site dating back to the 14th century. (In Hopi, Homolovi means "place of the little hills.") At **Dead Horse Ranch State Park** (675 Dead Horse Ranch Rd., Cottonwood, 928/634-5283, https://azstateparks.com/dead-horse), check out nearly 2 miles (3 km) of accessible wilderness trails that loop around the park's waterways.

No matter where you find yourself in Arizona's untouched lands, take care to follow the **Leave No Trace principles** (https://lnt.org) of outdoors conservation and preservation.

Connect with...

39 Dip into hot springs

46 Cool off in secret swimming holes

52 Join a star party

41 Enjoy desert blooms and autumn leaves

Scenic Drives • Day Trips

Why Go: From spring wildflowers to fall leaves, nature's seasonal shifts make themselves known in Arizona in striking ways.

Where: See seasonal flora all over the state in a variety of parks and botanical gardens.

Timing: Fall colors start in September in the state's higher elevations; in the high desert, leaves change October through early November; the Sonoran Desert's cottonwood trees boast autumnal colors late November through early December. Wildflower season starts in February in lower elevations and lasts through April, or early May for mountainous areas. The Sonoran Desert cactuses bloom in June and July.

Have you ever seen an aspen forest aglow in color? Or the willowy petals of a cactus flower blooming at midnight? What about a cliff blanketed in purple lupines? These sights—each more arresting than the last—signal Arizona's change in seasons. While neither Phoenix nor Tucson has distinct demarcations of spring, summer, fall, or winter, with a little road-tripping, it's easy to stitch together a four-season experience.

The desert's rocky floor explodes with wildflowers in March, April, and May. Throughout the Sonoran Desert, look for lemony poppies, patches of fiddleneck, the sunflower-like desert chicory, and the red tubular flowers of the chuparosa. The hedgehog cactus lives in central and southern Arizona and sports fuchsia pink flowers in April. Around the same time, tiny red buds top the ocotillo (common in the Sonoran and Chihuahuan Deserts), pale purple flowers dot the branches of the ironwood tree, and yellow flowers cluster in brilliant bunches on the palo verde. **Oracle State Park** (3820 Wildlife Dr., Oracle, 520/896-2425, https://azstateparks.com/oracle), **Picacho Peak State Park** (I-10, exit 219, Eloy, 520/466-3183, https://azstateparks.com/picacho), and **Tucson Botanical Gardens** (2150 N. Alvernon Way, Tucson, 520/326-9686, https://tucsonbotanical.org) are the best places to go for spring flowers.

desert wildflowers in spring

cactus bloom

See the leaves change at Arizona Snowbowl in Flagstaff.

189

In the summer, make it a point to see the white blossom of the saguaro. It crowns the cactus in early June, opening its petals at night for bats to pollinate. June is also peak bloom for the magenta flowers of the cholla cactus, which grows between 500 and 2,500 feet in elevation in the Sonoran Desert. In July, the ceroid cactus's short-lived flower blooms at night, and only once a year. In Flagstaff, fields of sunflowers pop up in July and August. And August is when the thick pads of the prickly pear cactus ripen with fruit, ruby red on the outside, juicy on the inside. Head to **Desert Botanical Garden** (1201 N. Galvin Pkwy., Phoenix, 480/941-1225, www.dbg.org), which hosts nighttime events to watch the ceroid cactus flowers bloom, **Catalina State Park** (11570 N. Oracle Rd., Tucson, 520/628-5798, https://azstateparks.com/catalina), **Fort Valley Flower Field** (Fort Valley Road and Shultz Pass Road, Flagstaff), **Saguaro National Park** (3693 S. Old Spanish Trail, Tucson, 520/733-5153, www.nps.gov/sagu), and **Tohono Chul** (7366 Paseo del Norte, Tucson, 520/742-6455, www.downtowntempe.com/go/tempe-town-lake) for summer flora.

The spring-blooming ocotillo also sports flowers during fall, as does the cholla. But the real treat this time of year is autumn color. See the brilliant yellow and gold leaves of the aspens set against their stark-white trunks in Flagstaff. The best way: a scenic chairlift ride up the mountainside at **Arizona Snowbowl** (9300 N. Snowbowl Rd., Flagstaff, 928/779-1951, www.snowbowl.ski). Discover more aspen color, as well as the oranges leaves of the oaks, in the **White Mountains** (Show Low, Greer, Pinetop-Lakeside) during the first weeks of October. Colors peak later in the season (November) at **Boyce Thompson Arboretum** (37615 E. Arboretum Way, Superior, 520/689-2723, www.btarboretum.org) in Superior. The park's nearly 350 acres of trees—sycamores, cottonwoods—paint the scenery in reds and oranges. **Lockett Meadow** (northeast of Flagstaff on US 89, left on FR 552, right at Lockett Meadow sign, www.fs.usda.gov/recarea/coconino), **Red Rock State Park** (4050 Red Rock Loop Rd., Sedona, 928/282-6907, https://azstateparks.com/red-rock), and **Sunrise Park Resort** (200 Hwy. 273, Greer, 855/735-7669, www.sunriseskipark.com) are also great spots to visit for fall color.

Wildflowers begin to bloom in the still-cool temperatures of February in the Prescott National Forest; spot lupine, brittlebush, and globemallow. Late winter kicks off the life cycle of the wispy gravel ghost, a delicate desert wildflower with thin, spindly stalks. Pushing up

Making It Official

The saguaro is Arizona's official state cactus, its snow-white bloom is our state flower, and the cactus wren—who makes a home inside the hollow ribs of the saguaro—is Arizona's official bird. The palo verde takes top honors as our state tree.

through the rock and sprouting in sandy areas of the desert, marigold flowers bloom November and early December. **Lost Dutchman State Park** (6109 N. Apache Trail, Apache Junction, 480/982-4485, https://azstateparks.com/lost-dutchman) and the **Prescott National Forest** (www.fs.usda.gov/prescott) are the best places to visit in winter.

The truth is, it doesn't matter what time of year you choose for seasonal exploration. Because it boasts a staggering range of diverse ecosystems and dramatic changes in elevation, Arizona gifts us with year-round outdoor beauty. As you adventure into the great wide open, keep in mind the **Leave No Trace principles.** To tailor these to our state's unique geography, Visit Arizona partnered with the Leave No Trace Center for Outdoor Ethics to help promote sustainable enjoyment of Arizona's landscapes. For helpful tips and useful hints, check out www.visitarizona.com/leave-no-trace.

Connect with...

48 Drive the Joshua Tree Parkway
49 Pack up for a family campout
51 Pick saguaro fruit

42 Trek the Arizona Trail

Outdoor Adventures • Weekend Getaways

Why Go: The Arizona Trail (AZT) is one of fewer than a dozen long-distance trails in the United States to earn the National Scenic Trail designation.

Where: Arizona Trail Association • 602/252-4794, www.aztrail.org

Timing: It takes 6-8 weeks to thru-hike the trail from south to north. Only about 100 people each year attempt this; most choose to tackle individual passages as seasonality and schedules allow. For the southern passages, aim for fall and winter; for the northern routes, spring and summer are best. In October, join "AZT in a Day," an event where hundreds of hikers station themselves throughout the trail, each hiking several miles in order to complete—as a group—the whole trail in a single day.

One May morning in Phoenix, my husband and I packed up our dogs and drove to Flagstaff. It was one of those "spring" days that feels more like late June—searing hot and bone dry. We weren't ready to accept summer's advent, so we escaped north.

Our plan: to hike a segment of the **Arizona National Scenic Trail** (AZT), whose 43 passages along 800 miles (1,287 km) from Mexico to Utah we were slowly ticking off our to-do list. We opted for Passage 34 through the San Francisco Peaks. The length runs 36 miles (58 km) point to point, but we mapped a moderate 8-mile (13-km) round-trip route from Aspen Corner to the volcanic crater of Bismarck Lake.

(Fun fact: Those who complete the AZT, either at once or in sections, receive a copper belt buckle from the Arizona Trail Association.)

Among the 11 National Scenic Trails, the AZT isn't as long as some of its super-trail siblings. The Continental Divide Trail stretches 3,100 miles (4,989 km). The Appalachian Trail clocks in at 2,190 miles (3,524 km). But the AZT isn't the shortest either. That distinction goes to the 65-mile (105-km) Natchez Trace.

Together, these trails crosshatch the United States, from the surf of Long Island Sound to the pine-shrouded mountains of our very own state. Though they differ in length and

The Arizona Trail stretches from Mexico to Utah.

Passage 34 through Flagstaff is a tree-studded route.

terrain, the trails share the goal of, as the National Park Service describes, "showcasing our country's spectacular natural resources and beauty."

And that they do. Especially the AZT. Its passages—some less than 10 miles (16 km), others nearly 40 miles (64 km)—braid a path through a veritable "best of" Arizona backcountry.

Starting at the U.S.-Mexico border, the AZT passes through Grand Canyon National Park, Vermilion Cliffs National Monument, several state parks, and diverse biomes like the largest stand of ponderosa pines in the world, deep river gorges, lush riparian corridors, vast deserts, and its highest point, the 9,148-foot Kaibab Plateau. As Arizona's north-south backbone, the AZT connects communities, landmarks, and wilderness areas.

Flagstaff teacher Dale Shewalter first dreamed up the idea of the AZT in the 1970s. He envisioned a trail along the length of the state, and in 1985, to prove such a path was possible, he solo hiked from Mexico to Utah.

Trail construction began not long after, in 1988. With the combined efforts of Shewalter,

Reavis Ranch along the Arizona Trail in the Superstition Wilderness

Hike Inspiration

Following in the trail-to-book tradition of Cheryl Strayed's *Wild* about the Pacific Crest Trail or *A Walk in the Woods*, Bill Bryson's Appalachian Trail ruminations, comes a tiny tome called **Memorizing Shadows.** While hiking the AZT, Heidi Elizabeth Blankenship wrote poems, doodled art, and noted fleeting thoughts, then bundled them into this delightful book ($14.95, https://aztrail.org/product/memorizing-shadows).

the U.S. Forest Service, Bureau of Land Management, National Park Service, Arizona State Parks, and the tireless work of volunteers, the AZT morphed into epic shape. It earned its National Scenic Trail designation in 2009.

On our Passage 34 hike, we followed a footpath snug with dense aspen forests that broke open into alpine meadows with expansive views of Agassiz Peak and Humphreys Peak. Though hot in the Valley, here it was blissfully cool—we glimpsed mounds of snow in tight little packs, unthawed yet from winter, and stark tree branches just beginning to sprout green buds. The path was well maintained, but we saw nary another soul. Just us and the profound beauty of the wild.

(For safety information, please see page 187.)

Connect with...

40 Backpack the backcountry
47 Hike the hoodoos at Chiricahua National Monument
50 Wander lavender fields

43 Go wine-tasting

Drink and Dine • Scenic Drives • Day Trips

Why Go: A wine-tasting getaway promises sips of Arizona's award-winning wine, of course, but it also offers an excuse to explore some of Arizona's most beautiful landscapes.

Where: Sonoita and Elgin wine country, www.sonoitaelginchamber.org/wineries • Verde Valley wine country, https://vvwinetrail.com • Willcox wine country, https:// willcoxwinecountry.org

Timing: Plan for two days with an overnight stay. Tucson is closer to the wine countries of Sonoita/Elgin and Willcox; Phoenix is closer to the Verde Valley. From Tucson, it's 52 miles (84 km) south to Sonoita/Elgin; 83 miles (134 km) east to Willcox; and 216 miles (348 km) north to the Verde Valley. From Phoenix, it's 103 miles (166 km) north to the Verde Valley; 161 miles (259 km) to Sonoita/Elgin; and 195 miles (314 km) to Willcox. Note that weekends get busy at the wineries—especially in the Verde Valley—so if you can swing a midweek excursion, I strongly suggest it.

Arizona wine has come a long way. By that I don't mean it was once bad and now it's good. It's always been good. What I mean is now our wine-growing regions are getting the national recognition they deserve. Like Page Springs Cellars' Colibri Syrah Clone 174, which was the first Arizona wine to garner 90 points from Wine Spectator. Or the three Double Gold medals from the San Francisco Chronicle for Pillsbury Wine's Guns and Kisses red blend.

With so many recent accolades for established wineries, plus new wineries popping up, it can be hard to know where to start on an Arizona wine-tasting trip.

First thing: There are three wine countries in Arizona: Sonoita and Elgin, the Verde Valley, and Willcox. Second thing: You don't have to know anything. Wine tasting isn't about being a connoisseur. It's about learning and asking questions and trying new things. Arizona's wine industry is laid-back and friendly, so relax and enjoy yourself.

Sonoita and Elgin have close to 15 tasting rooms between them, but if you have to narrow down your stops to three, go with Los Milics Vineyards, Dos Cabezas WineWorks, and Callaghan Vineyards.

Welcome to Callaghan Vineyards.

treats from Page Springs Cellars

a taste from the cask at Dos Cabezas WineWorks

Los Milics Vineyards (423 Upper Elgin Rd., Elgin, 707/293-8480, https://losmilics-vineyards.com, Thurs.-Sun.) shows off the wines of Pavle Milic, who you may know from **FnB** fame (7125 E. 5th Ave., Scottsdale, 480/284-4777, www.fnbrestaurant.com, Wed.-Sat., $28). **Dos Cabezas WineWorks** (3248 AZ 82, Sonoita, 520/455-5141, www.doscabezas.com, Thurs.-Mon.) highlights earthy reds, but my favorite is the Pink, a blush blend of Garnacha, Syrah, and Piquepoul. And don't miss **Callaghan Vineyards** (336 Elgin Rd., Elgin, 520/455-5322, www.callaghanvineyards.com, Thurs.-Sun.), especially their Love Muffin white blend.

If you want to stay in town, **Dos Cabezas** offers a two-bed Casa NextDoor ($250/night) or a one-bed Casita NextDoor ($150/night), both equipped with a kitchenette, patio, and vineyard access.

Verde Valley has nearly 25 tasting rooms throughout Camp Verde, Clarkdale, Cornville, Cottonwood, Jerome, and Sedona. The following are my favorites.

You're in good hands with the knowledgeable staff at **Arizona Stronghold Vineyards** (1023 N. Main St., Cottonwood, 928/639-2789, www.azstronghold.com, noon-7pm Sun.-Thurs., noon-9pm Fri.-Sat.), who will guide you through a tasting of bold reds.

Carlson Creek Vineyards (1010 N. Main St., Cottonwood, 928/634-3866, www.carlsoncreek.com, 11am-7pm Sun.-Thurs., noon-9pm Fri.-Sat.) grows their grapes in southern Arizona and has three tasting rooms. The location in Cottonwood features live music in an airy space.

Page Springs Cellars (1500 N. Page Springs Rd., Cornville, 928/639-3004, https://pagespringscellars.com, 11am-7pm Sun.-Fri., 11am-9pm Sat.) is a favorite for many reasons: sustainable farming, dedicated conservation efforts, community activism, and a picturesque setting on the Verde River.

Staying in Verde Valley? Check into one of six rooms at the boutique boardinghouse, **The Clinkscale** (309 Main St., Jerome, 928/634-5094, www.theclinkscale.com, $209/night), within walking distance of Jerome's cluster of tasting rooms.

You'll find nine tasting rooms in **Willcox,** a quaint hamlet flanked by the Chiricahua Mountains. Pillsbury, Bodega Pierce, and Keeling Schaefer are the top spots.

Pillsbury Wine (1012 N. Main St., Cottonwood, 928/639-0646, 2pm-7pm Mon.-Thurs.,

Wine 101

Sisters Shaunna Cooper and Shayla Smith launched the wine education venture **Wine Spencer** (https://winespencer.com) in the hopes of redefining wine, especially for BIPOC communities and other groups traditionally not catered to by the wine industry. Phoenix-based Cooper and New York-based Smith lead a series of classes that touch on topics such as Black winemakers, a deep dive into red wine, and a tasting of South African wines.

noon-7pm Fri.-Sun., and 6450 S. Bennett Pl., Willcox, 928/595-1001, 11am-5pm Fri.-Sun.; www.pillsburywine.com) serves their lauded wines in tasting rooms in Willcox and Cottonwood, but the Willcox outpost is closest to the vineyards.

At **Bodega Pierce** (4511 E. Robbs Rd., Willcox, 602/320-1722, www.bodegapierce. com, noon-5pm Thurs.-Sun.), try the fragrant Malvasia Bianca or the plummy merlot.

Keeling Schaefer Vineyards is a mainstay on the Arizona wine scene, so don't skip a visit to their tasting room (154 N. Railroad Ave., Willcox, 520/766-0600, www.keelingschaefervineyards.com, 11am-5pm daily), located in the historic 1917 Willcox Bank and Trust. Their Rhone-style wines range from lively whites to full-bodied reds.

If you want to stay in Willcox, opt for the pet-friendly **Dreamcatcher Bed & Breakfast** (13097 AZ 181, Pearce, 520/824-3127, www.dreamcatcherbnb.com, $105/night), situated on 27 tree-covered acres.

Connect with...

🔄 Enjoy desert blooms and autumn leaves
🔄 Follow the Salsa Trail
🔄 Hike the hoodoos at Chiricahua National Monument

44 **Follow the Salsa Trail**

Drink and Dine • Scenic Drives • Weekend Getaways

Why Go: A scenic road-trip itinerary built completely around food? Yes, please!

Where: The various locations along the trail can be found throughout Graham and Greenlee Counties • 928/428-2511, www.grahamchamber.org/world-famous-salsa-trail.html

Timing: With centrally located Safford as base camp for the weekend, spend two days visiting more than a dozen Mexican restaurants. From Tucson, it's a two-hour drive to Safford; from Phoenix, it's three hours. The Salsa Trail hosts the annual Salsa Fest in September, a three-day party in Safford with salsa-eating contests, cooking demonstrations, and live entertainment.

Beer. Wine. Bourbon. Cheese. Chocolate. If it's worth sipping or sampling, there's probably a trail for it.

In Arizona, we have the **World Famous Salsa Trail,** a self-guided driving loop dotted with family-owned restos whose chefs dice, chop, and stir up the most incredible salsas you'll ever taste. How was it determined to be "world famous?" No idea. But who am I to argue with a mouth full of homemade chips and dip?

The basics of salsa are simple. Chunks of tomatoes, onions, and peppers combine to make a spicy sauce. Then creative choices must be made. Tempering the spice with sweet mango, throwing in a jalapeño, swirling in black beans. And cilantro—yay or nay?

Launched in 2005, the Salsa Trail traces the Old West Highway (U.S. 70) through Pima, Thatcher, Safford, and Solomon, then goes north to Morenci or south to Willcox. The trail comprises 13 Mexican-food restaurants, each offering their own takes on salsa.

A word to the wise: Come hungry. The trail is more than just tomato sauce. Each of these eateries has robust menus featuring tasty breakfast, lunch, and dinner dishes. It's almost like the salsa is an afterthought. (Almost.)

Get ready for the heat of a chile pepper in salsa.

Salsa comes in all different flavors.

Enjoy authentic Mexican food at restaurants on the Salsa Trail.

When you arrive in Safford, stop by the Graham County Chamber of Commerce to pick up local guides and maps. Then hit the road.

Casa Mañana (502 S. 1st Ave., Safford, 928/428-3170, https://casacrave.com, $10) opened in 1951 and has been serving original family recipes ever since. The creamy chicken enchilada comes with a crispy bean tostada, but the local favorite is rellenos with Hatch chiles.

Another local favorite is **El Coronado** (409 W. Main St., Safford, 928/428-7755, $10), where the huevos enchiladas are thick with layers of melty cheese, and the green salsa is fresh and cool.

In the small town of Solomon, everything at **La Paloma** (5183 E. Clifton St., 928/428-2094, $12) is delicious, from the zesty margaritas to the perfectly charred elote. Start with a classic cheese crisp, then go right for the ceviche in the honey-jalapeño-lime vinaigrette.

Another don't-miss stop on the trail is **La Unica Restaurant & Tortilleria** (142 N. Haskell Ave., Willcox, 520/384-0010, https://launica.squarespace.com, $14) for buttery soft

Tomatoes are the hero ingredients in salsa.

Where to Stay

In Safford, bed down for the night at the **Cottage Bed & Breakfast** (1104 S. Central Ave., 928/428-5118, http://cottagebedandbreakfast.com, $130/night), a quaint, 1890s-era hotel where the sweet aroma from the B&B's bakery awakens you each morning.

tortillas, plump tortas, and tender chicken mole. La Unica also offers a well-curated wine and spirits menu, with local vino from southern Arizona's wine country.

Full disclosure: My palate prefers a mild zip; no adrenaline-spiking spice for me. Even though I'm not a thrill-seeker when it comes to heat, I was impressed on the trail by how an expertly made salsa can highlight a chile pepper's unique flavor. The smokiness of a chipotle, for example, or the citrusy notes of a serrano, the habanero's hint of fruit, the earthiness of a Hatch chile.

Beyond learning the nuances of a chile pepper, there was also another trail takeaway. To appreciate this very Arizona regional specialty—or to appreciate anything, anywhere, anytime—try everything once and always keep an open mind.

Connect with...

🥄 Savor Sonoran-style food
🍷 Go wine-tasting

45 Haunt a ghost town

Day Trips • Art and Culture • Local Scenes

Why Go: Arizona's ghost towns are living museums of the state's storied past, an on-the-ground glimpse at everything from mining history to the glory days of Route 66.

Where: Some ghost towns are located in remote areas and require a two- to three-hour drive one way from Phoenix or Tucson. Others are located on the outskirts of metro areas and can be visited within an hour's drive.

Timing: Visit Arizona's ghost towns year-round.

I love a good ghost town. The ruins of a once bustling but now forgotten city—a school with a weed-ravaged playground, a cracked swimming pool at an abandoned motel—tells partial stories and half-truths. Your imagination fills in the rest.

△ Two Guns ghost town

In Arizona we have many faded vestiges of the past. Most were former mining communities that emptied overnight, townspeople leaving tins of food in pantries and shoes in closets. Others are the skeletons of tourist stops along Route 66, which shuttered when Interstate 40 paved through.

Some hide isolated in the middle of nowhere. Some neighbor major thoroughfares. All invite intrepid exploration. Over the years, I've traveled rutted-out roads and hiked forested trails to see as many of these time capsules as possible. Here are four of my favorites.

Kentucky Camp (www.fs.usda.gov/recarea/coronado/recarea/?recid=80620), near Sonoita, was founded by gold miners in the Santa Rita Mountains in 1874. When the gold ran out by the mid-1880s, the town's population dwindled from 500 miners to a small handful of people. Kentucky Camp was all but abandoned by 1910. The U.S. Forest Service has owned and operated the land since 1989; today, a volunteer caretaker lets visitors wander (no tours, you're on your own) the remaining five buildings: the assay office, the main headquarters,

a former camp structure at Two Guns ghost town near Winslow

the assay office at Vulture City near Wickenburg

two cabins, and an old barn. The adobe cabins sit on the edge of the 340-acre site, with the barn and headquarters holding center court. Dotted about you'll find rusted mining equipment and even a car, weeds choking its fragile, 100-year-old frame. You can tent camp just outside the gates or, as part of the Forest Service's "Room with a View" program, you can overnight on-site in a cabin ($75/night) with a wraparound plank porch.

Another mining town, **Ruby** (http://rubyaz.com), near Arivaca, burst onto the scene in 1877 with vast stores of zinc, lead, and copper. It fared far better (and longer) than Kentucky Camp, hitting its production stride in the 1930s. Because of this, Ruby was a fully realized town with a post office, hospital, jail, mercantile shop, and schoolhouse. However, when the mine closed in 1940, it didn't take long for Ruby's 1,200 residents to flee; the town was completely empty within a year. A caretaker lives in a trailer on the town's hillside now. When you enter the grounds, drive there first to pay an admission fee ($12/person, cash only). Park near the sandy tailings at Mineral Lake, a beautiful, canyon-walled body of water that abuts Ruby. Then embark on a self-guided tour of 25 intact structures, from the school (peek in the windows to see the blackboards hanging bare) to miners' homes where kitchen chairs lie overturned and dusty mason jars line the shelves.

Zooming from Flagstaff to Winslow on I-40, you'll pass a dilapidated cluster of structures on the south side of the highway. At first glance, they look to be remnants of an ancient pueblo. But then you'll see etched into the stone an old sign advertising "Mountain Lions" and a gutted gas station—decidedly not ancient. This is **Two Guns** (I-40, exit 230), a former Mother Road outpost. Route 66 opened in 1926, and to lure motorists to stop and spend their money, Harry Miller built a soda shop, a zoo (with the aforementioned mountain lions), and fake American Indian ruins. These "ruins" were constructed on the site of a fatal Apache-Navajo fight in 1878 where 42 Apache men died, a fact that many believe led to the curse of Two Guns. After suffering attacks from the lions, two fires, and a violent dispute with a nearby landowner, Miller left town. By the late 1970s, Two Guns had fallen into disrepair. Still standing today are the gas station, a graffiti-covered swimming pool, the zoo, and the fake ruins.

Though the most productive gold mine in Arizona history is no longer in operation as a mine, **Vulture City** (36610 355th Ave., Wickenburg, 877/425-9229, www.vultureminetours.com) maintains popular appeal as a well-preserved mining town. From 1863 to 1942, the

Ghost Hunting Preparedness

With the exception of Vulture City, these ghost towns offer little to no services. Two Guns, Ruby, and Kentucky Camp do not have stores at which to purchase water, snacks, or souvenirs, so pack a cooler with food and drinks for the trip. Two Guns and Ruby also don't have bathrooms; Kentucky Camp does. You'll need a high-clearance vehicle to access the ruts of the dirt road to Ruby, but passenger vehicles are fine for the others. Plan ahead and gas up before your trip.

mine produced 340,000 ounces of gold and 260,000 ounces of silver, and at its peak, Vulture City was home to 5,000 residents. The mine has actually been credited with helping found the nearby (non-ghost) town of Wickenburg. Today, Vulture City offers visitor-friendly amenities such as guided tours ($15/person) of 12 meticulously restored buildings—many full of original furniture and artifacts—and picnic tables for post-tour lunches.

Connect with...

36 See wild horses along the Salt River

39 Dip into hot springs

48 Drive the Joshua Tree Parkway

46 Cool off in secret swimming holes

Outdoor Adventures • Day Trips

Why Go: Hidden coves, cool creeks, and spring-fed pools—these are the sought-after spots for Phoenicians and Tucsonans when the blazing hot days of summer stretch long and endless.

Where: Check out Bridal Wreath Falls, Bull Pen, Reavis Falls, and Wet Beaver Creek.

Timing: In Arizona, natural swimming holes are dependent on rainfall and snow-melt. March through May are the best times to take advantage, although August monsoons can bring heavy rain as well. To ensure you enjoy generous water flows, check weather conditions first. Plan for 90 minutes to two hours of drive time, then an hour of hike time.

Even though most of us in Phoenix and Tucson have a swimming pool—or we know somebody with a swimming pool—there's something more satisfying about splashing around in a natural oasis. Maybe it's the vigorous hike to reach the destination. Maybe it's the shared camaraderie of strangers stumbling upon the same secret spot. Maybe it's just hot and we need an icy dip.

Whatever the reason, I know this: As soon as the temperature starts to creep up, my husband and I grab our bathing suits and our dogs and head for Arizona's creeks and canyons.

The closest swimming spot to Phoenix is **Reavis Falls** (602/225-5395, www.fs.usda.gov/detail/tonto), near Apache Junction. It's also the least reliable in terms of water flow due to its location in the desert environs of the Superstition Wilderness. But if winter rain has been plentiful, you're in for a treat. Reavis Falls plunges 190 feet in a cascade of water over boulders and alongside juniper trees, feeding the stream that runs beside the trail. Because the out-and-back trek is 13 miles (21 km), you'll enjoy the falls pretty much to yourself. To get there from Phoenix, take U.S. 60 east, then drive northeast on AZ 88. After 25 miles (40 km) of paved and dirt roads, turn right at Reavis Ranch to access the trailhead.

 ▵ embankment of Wet Beaver Creek

 ▵ a hammock near Wet Beaver Creek

 ▵ the still, tranquil waters of Wet Beaver Creek

One of the deepest pools for swimming and diving is **Bull Pen** (928/203-2900, www. fs.usda.gov/recarea/coconino), a watering hole in West Clear Creek near Camp Verde. Hike the 9-mile (14 km) West Clear Creek Trail to the pool's rocky shores, where depths can measure nearly 10 feet down. Along the way you'll crisscross the stream several times; cool off in the pools and slickrock waterslides. To find Bull Pen, drive I-17 north from Phoenix to AZ 260. Go east on AZ 260 for 8 miles (13 km) to Forest Road 618. Turn left and take FR 618 for 2 miles (3 km) to FR 215. Turn right and drive 3 miles (5 km) to the trailhead.

Wet Beaver Creek (928/203-2900, www.fs.usda.gov/recarea/coconino) is a not-so-secret swimming hole in Sedona, but it still makes the list for being a near-perfect getaway. Tucked into a red-rock canyon is what's affectionately known as The Crack, a cold, clear pool. Cliff-jumping from the sandstone rocks is popular, but if you're more of a float-on-your-back kind of swimmer, there's plenty of room for that, too. Follow Bell Trail 3.5 miles (6 km) to the lush riparian destination. From Phoenix, take I-17 north to exit 298. Exit and drive 2 miles (3 km) east on Forest Road 618 to the Bell Trail trailhead.

▲ After spring thaw, the waters rage at Wet Beaver Creek.

Thousands of saguaros lead the way to **Bridal Wreath Falls** (520/733-5153, www.nps. gov/sagu), near Tucson. Located in the Rincon Mountain District of Saguaro National Park (3693 S. Old Spanish Trail, Tucson), Bridal Wreath's delightful grotto is shaded by cottonwood trees and looming canyons. As with Reavis, the falls' flow depends on recent rains. I've seen the waters of Bridal Wreath tumbling down 20 feet and I've also seen them run completely dry. No matter, the 5.7-mile (9 km) out-and-back Douglas Spring Trail rates as moderate, is well marked, and offers wonderful views of the national park's namesake wonder.

Because these swimming holes require a little legwork to reach them, you'll want to be prepared. Bring a daypack stocked with a bathing suit, sunscreen, towel, water shoes, light jacket or layers, extra pair of hiking socks, water, snacks, map, GPS navigation, small flashlight, and an emergency kit. For the hike, wear pants or shorts, a sun-reflective shirt, a wide-brimmed hat, and sturdy hiking shoes.

Connect with...

🔞 Ply the waters of Tempe Town Lake
㉛ Summit "A" Mountain at sunrise
㊾ Join a star party

47 Hike the hoodoos at Chiricahua National Monument

Outdoor Adventures • Weekend Getaways

Why Go: Walk among the hardened ash "ruins" of a volcanic eruption 27 million years old—rock spires towering hundreds of feet high, caves in mountainsides, and ancient lava flows etching the land.

Where: Chiricahua National Monument is located 120 miles (193 km) southeast of Tucson. Take I-10 east from Tucson to the first exit for Willcox. Travel 3 miles (5 km) to the stoplight. Turn right. Follow AZ 186 for 32 miles (52 km) to AZ 181. Turn left. Drive 4 miles (6 km) to the park entrance. • 520/824-3560, www.nps.gov/chir

Timing: Chiricahua National Monument (free) is open year-round. The visitor center is open 8:30am-4:30 pm daily and offers day-hiking guides. The best time of year to visit is March-May and September-October, when temperatures hang out at a comfortable mid-60s to low 80s. Summers can be hot (albeit cooler than Phoenix and Tucson) with temperatures in the low 90s; monsoon storms rage in July and August. Snowstorms occur November to early spring, although because of the mild temperatures (highs in the 50s), winter snow melts quickly.

Gnarly and knobby, craggy and jagged, the volcanic-formed rock pinnacles of **Chiricahua National Monument** lend themselves to a generosity of adjectives that still somehow defy an accurate description. I remember once saying they looked like plump macaroons piled on top of one another. Yum.

Known as hoodoos, the rhyolite spires rise together to form rock forests, each tower thick with layered sediment. The natural formations balance—precariously—and lead like cookie crumbs deep into the 12,000-acre park.

It's here, in the "Wonderland of Rocks," that you'll have your pick of 17 miles (27 km) of hiking trails (thanks to the 1930s-era Civilian Conservation Corps), specifically designed to offer hikers the best possible views of the park's natural features. Whether you're looking for an easy stroll or a strenuous backcountry adventure—or a meandering scenic drive—you'll find it here, and with no shortage of otherworldly vistas.

The 1.2-mile (1.9 km) Silver Spur Meadow Trail traces the ephemeral Bonita Creek

Snow caps the hoodoos.

Organ Pipe rock formation at Chiricahua National Monument

Rocks do a balancing act at Chiricahua National Monument.

from Faraway Ranch. This was the homestead of the Erickson family, Swedish immigrants who settled the land. They founded the ranch in the early 1900s; today, you can see several preserved structures, including the log-built Stafford Cabin. Follow the trail to its conclusion at the visitors center.

For a moderate hike that gets you into the magnificent rock scenery, try the 3.3-mile (5.3 km) Echo Canyon Loop. The two-hour trek combines the Echo Canyon, Hailstone, and Ed Riggs Trails, and shows off famous formations like the Grottoes and Wallstreet. Yuccas and prickly pear cacti give way to dense stands of big pine trees. Despite the change in vegetation, the elevation gain is less than 500 feet.

Experienced backpackers with a sense of adventure (and eight hours to kill) should opt for the Heart of Rocks Trail (7.3 miles/11.7 km round-trip). Starting at the visitors center, you'll traverse the lower canyon forest on the Rhyolite Canyon Trail, then start ascending the canyon to connect with the Sarah Deming Trail and the Heart of Rocks Loop. Get ready for iconic Chiricahua sights: Big Balanced Rock, Totem Pole, and Punch and Judy.

Happy Campers

You'll find lodging options in nearby Willcox (34 miles/55 km), but camping at Chiricahua is the way to go. The **Bonita Canyon Campground** (877/444-6777, www.recreation.gov, $20 per site, per night, reservations required) offers leafy shade during the day and star-studded skies at night, plus restrooms with flush toilets, potable drinking faucets, picnic tables, grills, and tent pads.

An accessible way to experience the magic of the Chiricahuas is the 8-mile (13 km) scenic drive that starts from the park entrance and circles up to roadside viewpoints like the 6,870-foot Massai Point, then follows the course of the stream through Bonita Canyon to showcase views of the Organ Pipe rock formation.

Connect with...

40 Backpack the backcountry
42 Trek the Arizona Trail
43 Go wine-tasting

48 Drive the Joshua Tree Parkway

Scenic Drives • Day Trips • Beautiful Views

Why Go: On a stretch of highway in the middle of nowhere stands one of the most stunning landscapes in the Southwest: a forest thick with Joshua trees that blanket the desert as far as the eye can see.

Where: From Phoenix, take I-17 north to AZ 74 (24 miles/39 km), then follow AZ 74 west to U.S. 60 (30 miles/48 km). Drive U.S. 60 northwest to Wickenburg (10 miles/16 km). Joshua Tree Parkway (U.S. 93) starts in Wickenburg. Drive north on U.S. 93 for 75 miles (121 km) to Wikieup.

Timing: Schedule 6-8 hours for this journey. You're looking at four hours in drive time (round-trip), and that doesn't include stops for gas, food, and soaking in the scenery. I suggest timing the trip so you reach the densest part of the forest—around milepost 169—as the sun is setting. Best time of year: March or April, when the wildflowers bloom.

When I first moved to Arizona, I was taken with the saguaro. A cactus alien in form and yet strangely humanlike—fat arms reaching out as if welcoming a hug, a white flower perched on top like a jaunty cap—its iconic pose captivated me. Then I saw my first Joshua tree.

Here's the thing about Joshua trees. Well, actually here are three things about Joshua trees: 1) They're not trees, in fact, but agave; 2) they're found nowhere else on Earth but in the Mojave Desert; and 3) they grow only within a narrow window of elevation from 2,000 to 4,000 feet.

Which is to say, they are wonderfully unique and highly specific to our nook of the world.

With twisted branches that culminate in globes of spiky leaves, the Joshua tree looks as though it was dreamed into existence by a surrealist painter or a

Joshua trees along Arizona's Joshua Tree Parkway

Arizona's Joshua trees

The Joshua Tree Parkway winds north from Wickenburg.

children's book author. In fact, many liken the plant to the baobab trees from Antoine de Saint-Exupéry's *The Little Prince* or the Truffula trees from Dr. Seuss's *The Lorax*.

Now imagine thousands of this odd and spectacular plant stretching for miles in every direction. That's the Joshua Tree Parkway.

The parkway starts as you drive U.S. 93 north out of **Wickenburg.** A worthy destination in and of itself, Wickenburg wears its Old West heritage proudly with the **Desert Caballeros Museum** (21 N. Frontier St., 928/684-2272, https://westernmuseum.org) and the former mine and ghost town of Vulture City (36610 355th Ave., 877/425-9229, www.vultureminetours.com). I recommend a stop at **The Local Presse Sandwich Bar** (69 N. Frontier St., 928/684-8955, https://sites.google.com/view/thelocalpress) to pick up road-trip sammies. My fave? The Mojo Cubano, roasted pork smothered in white cheddar and topped with pickled onions.

Once you begin winding up and over the hills out of Wickenburg, you'll find yourself in remote backcountry—craggy mountains, striated canyons, desert vistas. You won't be the only driver on the road, though, as this route is popular with Phoenix-to-Vegas weekenders.

As the parkway gains in elevation, the hallmarks of the Sonoran Desert give way to the Joshua trees of the Mojave. They pepper the sightline slowly, one or two at a time, but by **milepost 169,** you're surrounded on all sides. Highway signs spell out the obvious: "Welcome to the Joshua Tree Parkway of Arizona." Scenic pullouts on both sides of the road allow you to stop the car and stand among these weird desert denizens. This is also your best chance to capture photos.

As you continue north, look for the sculptural hoodoos popping up between the Joshua trees. At **milepost 147,** you approach Nothing, Arizona. The appropriately named "town" boasts a faded sign, an empty building, and some piles of gravel.

As you cross the Big Sandy River at **milepost 127,** sheer cliffs and stark canyon walls grant a dramatic backdrop to the Joshua trees. Keep driving to **Wikieup,** the endpoint of the parkway. It's here that you'll celebrate the epic journey with food and souvenirs from **Luchia's** (15797 U.S. 93, 928/765-2229) and an Insta snap at the **Snoopy Rocket.**

What's in a Name

According to the National Park Service, the Joshua tree gets its name from 19th-century Mormon immigrants. One theory is that when the pioneers saw the plant's limbs lifted as if in prayer, they named it after the biblical figure Joshua. Another theory is that the plant's sharp leaves reminded travelers of Joshua's army, and thus represented their "conquest" of the desert.

Connect with...

1 Take to the sky in a hot-air balloon

38 Dine in the desert

41 Enjoy desert blooms and autumn leaves

Pack up for a family campout

Outdoor Adventures • Fun for Families and Kids • Weekend Getaways

Why Go: See some of the top Arizona state parks on guided family outdoors trips that not only teach you and your little ones the basics of camping but also inspire a lifelong love of Arizona's natural landscapes.

Where: Arizona State Parks • 877/MY-PARKS (877/697-2757), https://azstateparks.com/family-camp

Timing: Arizona State Parks offers two-day weekend camping trips for families of four (additional members cost extra) at state parks all over Arizona, from Safford in the south and Payson in the north to Lake Havasu in the west. There's one session in September, two in October, three in November, and one in December.

When I was growing up, family vacations consisted of road trips along the eastern seaboard, where we visited relatives in New York and Pennsylvania or pilgrimaged to historic sites like Gettysburg or Washington DC. We were fortunate enough to travel by plane, too, jetting off to Disneyland in California and Yellowstone National Park in Wyoming.

The unifying factor of these family excursions was this: We always—always—stayed in hotels. No RVs or camper trailers for us, and definitely no tents. I was a kid weaned on room service, resort pools, and air-conditioned bedrooms, not the great outdoors.

When I became an adult and made other adult friends, I soon realized that not knowing how to roll a sleeping bag or roast a marshmallow placed me firmly in the minority. How had I gone 20-something years not knowing the simple rules of camping?

This is why I was delighted to hear about Arizona State Parks' **Arizona Family Campout Program.** Had I discovered this when I was 10 years old, I would have begged my family to sign up for one of the weekend sessions. These seasonal (Sept.-Dec.), guide-led camping trips ($90 for a family of 4, additional members cost $5 each) teach newbies everything they need to know about overnighting under the stars. To clarify, these aren't how-

1: An Arizona State Parks ranger leads happy campers. **2:** Slide Rock State Park **3:** Lake Havasu State Park **4:** Patagonia Lake State Park to-survive-in-the-wilderness classes; they're how-to-*enjoy*-the-wilderness classes. Which is sometimes difficult for us city slickers to do.

For seven weekends every autumn, an experienced ranger hosts a group of several families at different state parks. Past destinations have included **Tonto Natural Bridge State Park** (10 miles north of Payson, 928/476-4202, https://azstateparks.com/tonto), home of the world's largest travertine bridge; **Oracle State Park** (3820 Wildlife Dr., 520/896-2425, https://azstateparks.com/oracle), a renowned International Dark Sky destination near Tucson; and metro Phoenix's **Lost Dutchman State Park** (6109 N. Apache Tr., Apache Junction, 480/982-4485, https://azstateparks.com/lost-dutchman), where the famed—and never found—buried gold treasure lies.

In addition to receiving a thorough download on Camping 101 (how to pitch a tent, how to cook outside, how to safely start and extinguish a campfire), families participate in astronomy sessions, fishing clinics, mountain biking classes, live-animal demonstrations, guided

Roper Lake State Park

Get Inspired

Phoenix journalist Lisa Van Loo writes a fantastic blog called ***Raising Outdoor Kids*** (https://raisingoutdoorkids.com) in which she chronicles the nature expeditions of her and her partner's blended family of five kids. Her stories offer a great read and a source of inspiration for how to introduce your own family to the outdoors.

hikes, archery lessons, and presentations on area geography, geology, and wildlife. They even get a chance to work on a service project at the park.

For families that don't have, or can't afford, the gear required for a camping adventure, this program is ideal. Arizona State Parks provides everything: tents, sleeping mats, camp chairs, activity equipment, and first-aid kits. Families only need to bring their own food and personal items, bedding, clothing, shoes, water bottles, and flashlights.

It took me years to overcome my fears, both big and small, of the wild. But with every backpacking trip and every camping outing, I not only got more comfortable with nature but also more appreciative. And I think that's the real gift of this program. How can we preserve and protect something if we don't first care deeply about it?

Connect with...

7 Take a field trip on the Fresh Foodie Trail
20 Lace up your boots for an urban hike on Trail 100
41 Enjoy desert blooms and autumn leaves

50 Wander lavender fields

Day Trips • Scenic Drives

Why Go: Come for the sight of thousands of purple flowers rippling over the hills of Pine; stay for hands-on culinary classes, a gift shop stocked with goodies from the farm, and a chance to tour a pioneer homestead.

Where: Pine Creek Canyon Lavender Farm • 4223 Pine Creek Canyon Dr., Pine, 623/826-4717, www.pinelavenderfarm.com

Timing: If you're coming from Phoenix, a visit to Pine Creek Canyon Lavender Farm is a comfortable day trip. You're looking at a one-hour-and-45-minute drive (one way) north on AZ 87. For Tucsonans, the drive is three hours one way. Consider overnighting in Pine or Strawberry before returning home. The farm is open Friday-Monday.

Millions of years of erosion—and some dramatic faulting—formed the massive rock escarpment known as the Mogollon Rim. Spanning 200 miles from the New Mexico border to the town of Ash Fork in western Arizona, the Rim cleaves the state in half to form the southern cusp of the Colorado Plateau. Its rugged limestone walls scale thousands of feet high in areas, and above and below the Rim's edge hide all sorts of wonders: jagged canyons, crashing waterfalls, ponderosa pines, rolling meadows, pristine lakes, and a favorite of mine, **Pine Creek Canyon Lavender Farm.**

One of Arizona's most endearing qualities is its ability to constantly surprise. A wild and fragrant lavender farm tucked in the shadow of an ancient geologic formation? That fits the bill.

The farm is owned and operated by Terry Vesci, a former lawyer turned lavender whisperer, and her husband, Rick. Armed with a simple serrated tool curved like a scythe, the couple hand-harvests 5,000 lavender plants in fields spring-fed by the nearby waters of Pine Creek.

Pioneers first homesteaded the property as a corn and cattle farm in the late 1800s, but it sat dormant for decades. Terry and Rick purchased it from the family's original ancestors

The farm dog keeps watch over the lavender fields.

refreshing margaritas made with lavender

The lavender farm is an historic homestead.

and, since 2015, have spent years lovingly restoring the buildings and land. This includes planting and growing three varieties of lavender: Royal Velvet, Provence, and Grosso. The first two are culinary varieties, while Grosso is known for its aromatics.

Terry and Rick live in the original farmhouse, using the 1800s-era kitchen with its sunlit windows and book-filled nooks to host lavender cooking classes for visitors. Terry leads the classes, teaching would-be chefs how to mix, cook, bake, and stir with lavender. Recipes featuring the farm's lavender include everything from sweet treats to cocktails. Classes are held on the weekends and reservations are required ($40-70/person).

Also on the property sits an early 1900s hand-hewn log shed, which now enjoys a second life as the farm's gift shop. Drying lavender hangs from the rafters, and shelves stock the all-natural products (soaps, lotions, balms, and more) made from the farm's bounty. Visitors will also find culinary goods, such as lavender-lemon pepper (I use this on *everything*), lavender salt, lavender cream honey, and the ever-popular lavender cocoa.

When you visit, you're invited to walk among the lavender, breathing in the heady fra-

⌃ a summer day on the farm

226

The Arizona Trail

From the state's southern border to our northern Utah neighbors runs the epic, 800-mile (1,290 km) **Arizona National Scenic Trail** (for more, see page 192; https://aztrail.org). From the lavender farm, you're mere steps from Passage 26 of the trail, a shady hike that grants impressive Mogollon Rim vistas. Drive south of Pine on AZ 87 for a half mile, then turn left (east) to reach the trailhead.

grance and watching bees lazily buzz around the plants. If you see the couple's adorable dogs, stop and say hello.

It doesn't matter how often you visit the lavender farm, you'll always see something new, something different, something surprising. On a recent trip, I hung around the farm until dusk and lucked into the breathtaking sight of a dozen elk roaming the fields. The elk lumber down off the Mogollon Rim as the sun sets, moving their enormous bodies through the trees. I worried they would crush the delicate lavender. Not so. The animals move with a grace that belies their weight, and Terry says they never eat—much less touch—the plants. A surprising flora and fauna match, to be sure. But that's Arizona for you.

Connect with...

7 Take a field trip on the Fresh Foodie Trail
41 Enjoy desert blooms and autumn leaves
42 Trek the Arizona Trail

51 Pick saguaro fruit

Native Cultures • Weekend Getaways

Why Go: In the height of summer under a blazing sun, the ruby-red fruit of the saguaro—a plant found only in the Sonoran desert—blooms. On this guide-led journey, you can pluck it from its perch on top of the iconic cactus.

Where: 55 S. Orilla Ave., Ajo, 520/373-0804, www.sonorancc.com/calendar/saguaro-harvest-weekend

Timing: This weekend getaway is a two-day excursion in June. You'll spend a day on the harvest itself, and the rest of the time will be enjoyed learning how to cook with the saguaro fruit—complete with tastings! If you're coming from Phoenix, expect a two-hour drive to Ajo; from Tucson, it's about two hours and 15 minutes. Once you arrive at the Sonoran Desert Inn and Conference Center, all lodging, meals, and activities are taken care of.

The mighty saguaro stands as more than just an emblem of the Southwest, or a novelty icon emblazoned on T-shirts and spotlighted in old Western movies. It's a special plant. The cactus is only found in the Sonoran Desert, a biome that itself covers only Phoenix, Tucson, northern Mexico, and parts of California. It takes 70 years for a saguaro to grow a single arm. Small birds make their home inside its heavy body, and its spongelike roots can store water for years.

▲ saguaro fruit harvested by members of Tohono O'odham Nation

The saguaro's white flower blooms for a short week in May. In June, its pulpy fruit ripens. This is when the **Saguaro Harvest Weekend** happens. To say that joining the harvest is a once-in-a-lifetime event would be an understatement. Hosted by the **Sonoran Desert Inn and Conference Center** in Ajo, this event offers participants the rare chance to follow a guide—a member of the Tohono O'odham Nation—into the vast Organ Pipe Cactus National Monument to pluck the fruit from the top of the towering saguaro.

An Ancient Custom

To the Tohono O'odham people, saguaros are considered family—the Nation's great ancestors who are immortalized in traditional songs, ceremonies, and stories. The thousands-year-old practice of gathering fruit from the saguaro holds significance for the Tohono O'odham people because harvest marks the beginning of a new year. To express appreciation to their ancestors for the bounty—as well as the promise of rains to come—the Tohono O'odham people leave an empty fruit pod lying face up at the base of the saguaro after its fruit has been picked.

It's illegal to harvest the saguaro unless you're with a tribal guide. Enter Lorraine Eiler. Eiler is a member of the Hia C-ed O'odham community, which is related to the Tohono O'odham and Akimel O'odham people. She grew up in Ajo and spent endless days under the summer sun harvesting the saguaro, filling buckets with the dark red fruit. She's one of the founders of the **International Sonoran Desert Alliance,** a nonprofit group that aims to promote understanding of Native, Mexican, and Anglo cultures. Armed with a *kuipad* (a long stick fashioned out of the ribs of a dead saguaro and used to grab the fruit), she leads small groups into the desert during the weekend to harvest.

Saguaro fruit is juicy, with tiny black seeds, and it tastes like a pomegranate. Harvesting it is labor intensive, but fortunately you're teamed up into pairs for the weekend, each of you taking turns with the *kuipad*. After a day spent in the saguaro groves, you'll return to the Sonoran Desert Inn (your accommodations for the weekend) to apron up for cooking demonstrations. Highlights include learning how to wrap tamales and baking saguaro cookies. You'll also fashion your own *kuipad* and go on a guided tour of Ajo's murals.

Connect with...

7 Take a field trip on the Fresh Foodie Trail

14 Learn about Arizona's American Indian heritage at the Heard Museum

41 Enjoy desert blooms and autumn leaves

47 Hike the hoodoos at Chiricahua National Monument

52 Join a star party

Outdoor Adventures • Fun for Families and Kids • Beautiful Views

Why Go: Arizona claims more International Dark Sky sites than anywhere else in the United States. Escape the bright lights of the city at some of the best stargazing spots in the world.

Where: Visit Grand Canyon National Park, Kartchner Caverns State Park, Kitt Peak National Observatory Lowell Observatory for stargazing events.

Timing: Most nighttime viewing events kick off at sunset and are located outside urban areas. Depending on where you're going, plan for a two-hour drive one way. You can stargaze year-round—and you should, in order to see the constantly changing sky—but Grand Canyon National Park's star parties are only offered during the summer. Grand Canyon is also one of the most popular national parks in the country; if you plan to spend the night at the park, book reservations six months to a year in advance.

We're perhaps more famous for our sunsets, but Arizona also takes its night skies pretty seriously. And I'm not talking about amateur stargazing. Our state has thoughtful stewardship of communities, parks, and natural lands to keep them free of light pollution, as well as world-class observatories that spearhead cutting-edge research.

This has led to Arizona receiving nearly 20 International Dark Sky designations from the International Dark Sky Association (IDA). In fact, Arizona practically launched the movement to preserve dark skies when IDA designated Flagstaff the world's first Dark Sky Place in 2001.

So what is a Dark Sky Place? As defined by IDA, they are places with "exceptional quality of starry nights and a nocturnal environment that is specifically protected for its scientific, natural, educational, cultural heritage, and/or public enjoyment." This is achieved through lighting ordinances that set lumen limits and employ light curfews, and progressive lighting infrastructure such as shielding around bulbs.

Looking for an inky black sky punctuated with stars? You can find cosmic wonders as

Kitt Peak National Observatory perches high above the clouds.

International Dark Sky parks are excellent for stargazing.

Coming Soon

In 2024, Lowell Observatory will open a new Astronomy Discovery Center, which will feature a rooftop open-air planetarium. Picture a traditional planetarium sans roof—all the better to take advantage of Flagstaff's renowned dark skies.

soon as you drive outside the city, thanks to Arizona's mountainous terrain, which veils dark-sky spots from light pollution. But to *really* immerse yourself in celestial sights, I suggest a visit to an observatory or one of our International Dark Sky parks.

West of Tucson on the Tohono O'odham Nation perches **Kitt Peak National Observatory** (520/318-8720, https://visitkittpeak.org). Established in 1964, Kitt Peak is considered the country's first national observatory. It's home to the most diverse collection of research telescopes in the world, including the largest solar telescope. Of the nearly 25 active telescopes, 3 are open to the public for stargazing. Guided astronomy programs (from $55 per person) include Night of the Marvelous Moon, Dark Sky Discovery, and an introduction to dark-sky viewing.

Grand Canyon National Park's (South Rim, 60 miles north of Williams via AZ 64 from I-40, 928/638-7888, www.nps.gov/grca) 1.2 million acres of federally protected land are ideal for dark-sky exploration. It's one of nearly a dozen Arizona parks to earn an IDA Dark Sky designation. During the park's summer star parties ($35 per vehicle, valid for seven days), you might see Saturn or Jupiter, spot a meteor shower, or eye star clouds and nebulae. Star parties include telescope viewings and guest lectures.

More than 100,000 visitors drive Mars Hill annually to explore Flagstaff's **Lowell Observatory** (1400 W. Mars Hill Rd., Flagstaff, 928/774-3358, https://lowell.edu, $34-64 per person). Built in 1894 to initially study the planet Mars, Lowell gained infamy when, in 1930, astronomers discovered Pluto. Today the observatory offers dark-sky viewing through six telescopes on the Giovale Open Deck Observatory, plus educational programs, guided tours, interactive exhibits, and a chance to peek inside the Pluto Discovery Dome.

Another Arizona park with IDA Dark Sky status is **Kartchner Caverns State Park** (2980 S. Hwy. 90, Benson, 520/586-4100, https://azstateparks.com/kartchner), near Ben-

Celestial viewing doesn't get much better than at the Grand Canyon.

son. The park preserves "living" caves and limestone formations tucked underground in the Whetstone Mountains. On a clear night, you can see the Andromeda galaxy, planets like Mercury and Mars, star clusters, and intricate constellations. As part of Arizona State Parks' astronomy programming, Kartchner Caverns hosts star parties ($7 per vehicle) with lectures and telescope viewing.

Connect with...

42 Trek the Arizona Trail

47 Hike the hoodoos at Chiricahua National Monument

49 Pack up for a family campout

INDEX

PHOTO CREDITS

All photos © Jessica Dunham except: title page photo: Ian Adler; page 2 © (top) James Kelley | Dreamstime.com; (top middle) Derrick Neill | Dreamstime.com; (bottom) Sam Antonio | Dreamstime.com; page 3 © (top) Courtesy of Miss Gay Arizona America; (top middle) Courtesy of Wrigley Mansion; (bottom) Courtesy of MIM; page 4 © (top) Thomas Lohr | Dreamstime.com; (top middle) Courtesy of Return of the Mermaids; photo by Jeffrey Mead; (top middle) Scott Griessel | Dreamstime.com; (top middle) Scott Griessel | Dreamstime.com; (bottom middle) Henskier1 | Dreamstime.com; (bottom) Ronald Adcock | Dreamstime.com; page 5 © (top) Jonmanjeot | Dreamstime.com; (bottom middle) Courtesy of Arizona State Parks and Trails; page 14 © (top left) Jason Wilson; (top right) Sam Antonio | Dreamstime.com; page 15 © (top) Linda Johnsonbaugh | Dreamstime.com; page 16 © (top right) Catstyecam | Dreamstime.com; page 17 © (top left) Special for the Republic; (top right) Derrick Neill | Dreamstime.com; page 18 © (top left) Hpbfotos | Dreamstime.com; (top right) Gloria Anderson | Dreamstime.com; page 19 © (top left) Chon Kit Leong | Dreamstime.com; page 20 © (top) John Sirlin | Dreamstime.com; page 21 © (top left) Arizona Goat Yoga; GoatYoga.com; (top right) Courtesy of MIM; page 22 © (top left) Courtesy of Arizona Wilderness Brewing; (top middle) Danelle Mccollum | Dreamstime.com; (top right) Courtesy of Callaghan Vineyards; page 23 © (top left) Olivier Le Queinec | Dreamstime.com; (top right) Minacarson | Dreamstime.com; page 24 © (top right) Ian Adler; page 25 © (top) Paul Moore | Dreamstime.com; page 27 © (top left) James Kelley | Dreamstime.com; (top right) Greg Lightle | Dreamstime.com; (bottom) James Kelley | Dreamstime.com; page 28 © Gavin Walters | Dreamstime.com; page 31 © (bottom) Derrick Neill | Dreamstime.com; page 32 © Wirestock | Dreamstime.com; page 39 © (top) Chon Kit Leong | Dreamstime.com; (bottom) Chon Kit Leong | Dreamstime.com; page 40 © Chon Kit Leong | Dreamstime.com; page 47 © (bottom right) Courtesy of Arizona Wilderness Brewing; page 48 © Courtesy of Arizona Wilderness Brewing; page 51 © Courtesy of Visit Mesa; page 52 © Courtesy of Visit Mesa; page 55 © (top left) Special for the Republic; (top right) Special for the Republic; (bottom) Special for the Republic; page 56 © Special for the Republic; page 63 © Arizona Goat Yoga; GoatYoga.com; page 64 © Arizona Goat Yoga; GoatYoga.com; page 71 © (bottom) John Dvorak | Dreamstime.com; page 72 © (top) Danny Raustadt | Dreamstime.com; (bottom) Danny Raustadt | Dreamstime.com; page 75 © (top right) EasyArts | Dreamstime.com; (bottom) Brent Coulter | Dreamstime.com; page 76 © Gregory Clifford | Dreamstime.com; page 79 © (top left) Rebekah Zemansky | Dreamstime.com; (top right) Bdingman | Dreamstime.com; (bottom) Sam Antonio | Dreamstime.com; page 80 © Rebekah Zemansky | Dreamstime.com; page 83 © (top left) Jason Wilson; (bottom) Jason Wilson; page 84 © Jason Wilson; page 87 © (top) Courtesy of Miss Gay Arizona America; (bottom) Courtesy of Miss Gay Arizona America; page 88 © Courtesy of Miss Gay Arizona America; page 91 © (top) Danny Raustadt | Dreamstime.com; (bottom) Samet Arda | Dreamstime.com; page 92 © Tim Roberts Aerial | Dreamstime.com; page 95 © (top left) Hpbfotos | Dreamstime.com; (bottom) John Sirlin | Dreamstime.com; page 96 © Jeremy Christensen | Dreamstime.

ACKNOWLEDGMENTS

Narrowing the list in this book down to just 52 things was an impossible task. And that's a good thing. I am grateful to live in a place where people bring an adventurous, let's-try-anything entrepreneurial spirit to all that they do. Without the artists, business owners, chefs, makers, pioneers, athletes, musicians, writers, movers and shakers that comprise Tucson and Phoenix, life would be very boring indeed.

Thank you to Kim Ehart, my whip-smart editor who always offered spot-on suggestions and expertly shaped my sometimes-rambling thoughts into a cohesive book.

I want to thank Don and Diana Wilson for being the original travel guides in my life. From the first day I met them, they invited me on their family adventures around Arizona, showing me not just the beauty of this state, but also the kindness of its people.

To Nathan Wilson: I can't thank you enough for sharing your list of favorite things to do with me. Though sky-diving didn't make the final cut, your enthusiasm for living life to the fullest stays with me always.

To Ava Wilson: Your insightful questions during the writing process made this book so much better. I admire your creativity and thoughtful perspective on the world—you are welcome to be my editor any time.

Finally, thank you to my mom, Jerry Sorenson, and my husband Jason. They generously (and patiently) listened as I read chapter drafts aloud to them. My gratitude for their love and support has no limits.

MAP SYMBOLS

═══	Highway	①	Thing To Do	▲	Small Park
═══	Primary Road	⊛	National Capital	▲	Mountain Peak
═══	Secondary Road	◉	State Capital	✦	Unique Natural Feature
‥‥	Residential Road	○	City/Town	✦	Unique Hydro Feature
◻◻◻	Unpaved Road	✕	Airport	🌫	Waterfall
═══	Pedestrian Walkway	✕	Airfield		
‑‑‑‑	Trail				
▬▬▬	Paved Trail				
⋯⋯	Ferry				

CONVERSION TABLES

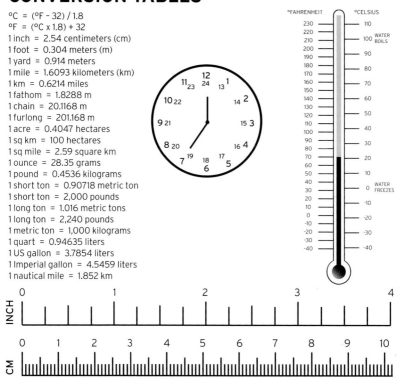

°C = (°F – 32) / 1.8
°F = (°C x 1.8) + 32
1 inch = 2.54 centimeters (cm)
1 foot = 0.304 meters (m)
1 yard = 0.914 meters
1 mile = 1.6093 kilometers (km)
1 km = 0.6214 miles
1 fathom = 1.8288 m
1 chain = 20.1168 m
1 furlong = 201.168 m
1 acre = 0.4047 hectares
1 sq km = 100 hectares
1 sq mile = 2.59 square km
1 ounce = 28.35 grams
1 pound = 0.4536 kilograms
1 short ton = 0.90718 metric ton
1 short ton = 2,000 pounds
1 long ton = 1.016 metric tons
1 long ton = 2,240 pounds
1 metric ton = 1,000 kilograms
1 quart = 0.94635 liters
1 US gallon = 3.7854 liters
1 Imperial gallon = 4.5459 liters
1 nautical mile = 1.852 km

MOON 52 THINGS TO DO IN PHOENIX & TUCSON

Avalon Travel
Hachette Book Group
1700 Fourth Street
Berkeley, CA 94710, USA
www.moon.com

Editor: Kimberly Ehart
Acquiring Editor: Nikki Ioakimedes
Series Manager: Kathryn Ettinger
Copy Editor: Ann Seifert
Graphics and Production Coordinator: Lisi Baldwin
Cover Design: Kimi Owens
Interior Design: Darren Alessi
Map Editor: Albert Angulo
Cartographer: John Culp

ISBN-13: 978-1-64049-635-4

Printing History
1st Edition — August 2022
5 4 3 2 1

Front cover photo: sunset at Tempe Town Lake SUP Adventures © Sarah Robinson / Almay Stock Photo

Back cover photos (clockwise from top): Return of Mermaids © Jeffery Mead; balloon soaring over desert © Greg Lightle | Dreamstime.com; frybread taco © Jessica Dunham; goat yoga © Arizona Goat Yoga's Goat Yoga.com; desert sunrise © Dianneslotten |Dreamstime.com (back flap) orchard dinner © Visit Mesa photo

Printed in Malaysia for Imago